Star
Family Walks

The Peak District & South Yorkshire

Walks & Text by John Spencer

Maps & illustrations by Ann Beedham

A CICERONE GUIDE

Location of walks

The number in the circle is the walk number

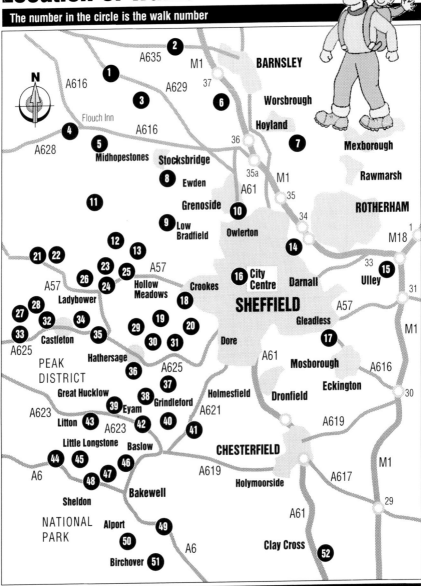

BARNSLEY

A635 M1
A616
A629 37
Worsbrough
Flouch Inn Hoyland
A616
Midhopestones Stocksbridge
Ewden A61 M1 35
Grenoside Rawmarsh
Low ROTHERHAM
Bradfield Owlerton
M18
A57 City
A57 Centre Darnall Ulley
Hollow Crookes 31
Meadows SHEFFIELD
Ladybower Gleadless
Castleton Dore M1
A625 Hathersage A625 A61 Mosborough A616
PEAK Eckington 30
DISTRICT Great Hucklow Holmesfield Dronfield
A623 Eyam Grindleford A619
Litton A623 A621
Little Longstone Baslow CHESTERFIELD
A6 A619 M1
Sheldon Bakewell Holymoorside A617
NATIONAL Alport A61 29
PARK A6 Clay Cross
Birchover

Mexborough

A628

35a

36

34

33

Sheldon

Maps used for the walks in this book:

Ordnance Survey Outdoor Leisure:
The White Peak
The Dark Peak

Ordnance Survey Pathfinder Series:
Numbers: 715, 726, 727, 743, 744, 779
Sheffield A - Z

Contents

© Copyright 1997
Sheffield Newspapers Ltd
York Street
Sheffield
S1 1PU

ISBN-13: 978 1 85284 257 4
ISBN-10: 1 85284 257 1

First published 1997
Reprinted 1999, 2002, 2005, 2009

Published by
Cicerone Press, 2 Police Square, Milnthorpe, Cumbria

Printed by KHL Printing, Singapore

Winner of the COLA/Outdoor Writer's Guild Award 1998
Best Guidebook Category

About the authors

J OHN Spencer is an editorial executive at The Star, Sheffield's evening newspaper, and has a keen interest in walking and natural history.

A NN Beedham has a degree in graphics and illustration, and worked in museums and design studios before her post as graphic artist at The Star. She shares an interest in walking and wildlife.

Together they produce The Star's Weekend Walk column, which appears every Saturday.

Star

Family Walks

The Peak District & South Yorkshire

A Year of Weekend Rambles

Walks by grade & distance

Choose the grade and mileage that suits your pace   A   B   C

No.	WALK TITLE	Grade	Mls	Page	No.	WALK TITLE	Grade	Mls	Page
1	Ingbirchworth Reservoir	A	2	1	27	Kinder from the South	C	6	27
2	Cannon Hall	A	4	2	28	Kinder Edge Walk	C	5	28
3	Penistone Circuit	A	5	3	29	Stanage Edge	A	4	29
4	Little Don	C	5	4	30	Carl Wark	C	4	30
5	Langsett Moors	A	4	5	31	Burbage Rocks	A	3	31
6	Wentworth Castle	A	3.5	6	32	Mam Tor Circuit	B	5	32
7	Wentworth & Elsecar	B	8	7	33	Rushup Edge	B	5	33
8	Scenic Bolsterstone	A	4.5	8	34	Hope Valley	A	3.5	34
9	The Bradfields & Agden	B	5	9	35	Roman Fort Walk	A	3	35
10	Grenoside Woods	A	4	10	36	Beside the Derwent	A	3	36
11	Howden Edge	C	6	11	37	Padley Gorge	A	4	37
12	Bradfield Moors	C	10	12	38	Froggatt Edge	A	4	38
13	Dale Dike Circuit	A	3	13	39	Historic Eyam	B	6	39
14	Sheffield & Tinsley Canal	A	4	14	40	White Edge	C	5	40
15	Ulley Country Park	A	2	15	41	Three Edges Circuit	A	5	41
16	Industrial Sheffield	A	2	16	42	North From Calver	B	6	42
17	The Moss Valley	A	3	17	43	Foolow	B	4	43
18	Redmires & Rivelin	B	4	18	44	Miller's Dale	B	5	44
19	Redmires Circuit	B	5	19	45	Monsal Dale	A	6	45
20	Mayfield Valley	A	3	20	46	Around Hassop	A	4	46
21	Seal Stones	C	5	21	47	Longstone Edge	B	3	47
22	Alport Castles	C	8	22	48	To Ashford	B	4	48
23	Derwent Edge	B	4	23	49	Wye Valley Round	A	5	49
24	Above Ladybower	B	4	24	50	Lower Lathkill Dale	A	4	50
25	Ughill Moor & Strines	A	5	25	51	White Peak Villages	C	9	51
26	Ladybower	A	4	26	52	Around Hardwick Hall	A	5	52

Introduction

It seems that rarely a week goes by without the launch of yet another walk book. Many try to aim their routes at the family, at small children even, but all parents know that what looks like a simple and easy outing can turn into a miserable route march with a bored or tired child.

In this book we have tried hard to choose routes which are both family friendly and interesting. Almost all of them can be done in the company of young children. Those few which are unsuitable are specifically marked, yet will still provide some energy sapping exercise for older youngsters who can be tempted away from the television and on to the hills. Testing them has involved carrying, cajoling and chasing my young son Tom - on many occasions only arming ourselves with plastic swords and turning the ramble into a Robin Hood style adventure has helped complete the round.

Although the text and maps should give you a feel of the route it must be emphasised that the diagrams are NOT intended as an accurate representation of the route on the ground. We have tried to give an impression of what will be encountered along the route, but one of the joys of walking is finding the way, with guidance from somebody who has been there before, of course.

The best way to use this publication is to choose your outing and then carefully consult the map indicated and locate the route on the ground. This not only helps ensure the way will be followed accurately, it helps identify escape routes in the case of bad weather, orientates the walker to appreciate the surroundings, and helps you devise your own short cuts.

Maps listed are of the Ordnance Survey Outdoor Leisure and Pathfinder series, to a scale of 250m per cm - ideal for route finding of this kind. I can't urge purchase of these too strongly, nor the need to know how to use a map and compass.

If this book helps just one more youngster appreciate the beauty on our doorstep it will have served its purpose.

Good Walking!

Sheffield, August 1997

What to take with you

Common Sense and experience

There is no secret about safe walking in the hills and mountains. Two items are indispensable, neither cost a thing and both can save your life - common sense and experience.

The former you are born with, the latter comes with time. Assuming we all have a modicum of common sense it makes it obvious that without experience to climb Kinder Downfall in winter and alone is to invite disaster.

Experience involves getting out on the tops as often as opportunity allows and slowly but surely attempting longer and more difficult routes; and always try to do so with a partner.

And although Mallory and Irving may have reached the summit of Everest in 1924 wearing puttees and Norfolk jackets, a range of more appropriate gear is now available for walkers.

Although the Peak is not the Himalaya, conditions can turn from benign to deadly in a short time.

Equipment for the walker

So what should we always take walking, apart from the essential map and compass discussed elsewhere?

First, wear a pair of decent boots which protect the ankle - and take a spare, dry pair of socks to change into after that first dunking in a peat grough. Always take a rucksack and in it pack a waterproof jacket and trousers, plus an additional fleece or jumper for when the weather gets rough.

Ensure you have a small first aid kit and a torch, ideally a head torch so that you have both hands free to study maps, rummage for food etc. On the subject of food, always take more than you think you will need, plus a hot drink.

Other essentials are a whistle to summon help and, another life saving "must", a survival bag. These are available from all outdoor shops for about £4 - choose one in bright orange, they are easiest to see from the air.

Lastly, and an item I swear by, is a waterproof "strobe" light. These are usually sold in scuba diving shops and for less than £20 provide a flashing light detectable by the right equipment in dense fog. Only switch it on when you need it, and pack a spare battery.

A few other tips

A good idea, especially in summer, is insect repellent. There are many types available. Lavender or citronella oil works too, but take care on clothes and plastic.

Keeping food cool in summer is a problem too. There are small sandwich size cool packs available in many stores and these are ideal to put in your rucksack. They are also good for medication that needs to be kept cool, such as diabetic insulin.

CHECK LIST

CLOTHES
Good boots
Spare socks
Rucksack
Waterproof jacket
Waterproof trousers
Fleece or jumper

EQUIPMENT
Map / Compass
First aid kit
Whistle
Strobe light
Survival bag
Torch

OTHER ITEMS
Food and drink
Insect repellent
Hand warmer
Sun tan lotion
Sunglasses
Ice packs

A strobe light, (left) ususally sold for scuba diving, is an excellent alert signal. It straps onto the body for easy use

How to use a compass

Sometimes - on moorland for example - paths are unclear and it may be necessary to choose a landmark, set a compass bearing and follow it in the right direction.

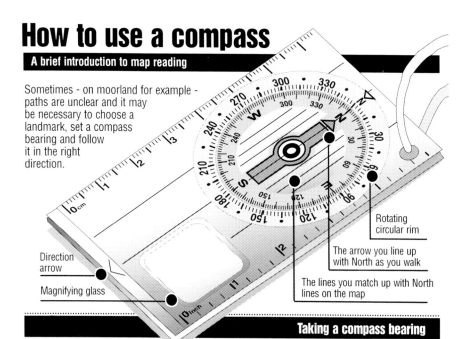

Direction arrow

Magnifying glass

Rotating circular rim

The arrow you line up with North as you walk

The lines you match up with North lines on the map

Taking a compass bearing

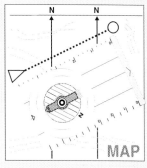

MAP

①

Place the compass on the Ordnance Survey map. Line the edge of it up along the route that you want to take

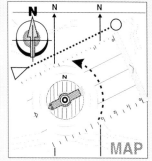

MAP

②

Turn the circular rim of the compass until the North arrow and lines on the compass are parallel with the vertical grid lines on the map

③

Pick up the compass. Turn your body round until the North end of the moving arrow lines up with North arrow printed on the compass rim.

The direction arrow printed on the compass base shows which way you should walk. Find something on the horizon to head towards so you don't need to keep looking at the compass. Once you reach it, find another and continue

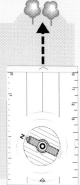

Walk in this direction, following the arrow on base of compass.

Find a land mark on the horizon to head towards

Key to symbols

 Distance
 Approximate time the walk takes
 Where to find public toilets
 Take a picnic

 Where to get refreshments
 Where the nearest public house is
 P Where to park

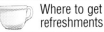 **MAP** **Which map is needed to help find your way on the walk** *Grid reference for start*

Walks suitable for almost any age, from an adult carrying a child in a "papoose" to youngsters aged four or five able to enjoy a reasonable stroll under their own steam and in their own time.

A little bit tougher, possibly requiring more time than initially expected when younger children are involved - or longer than average and probably only for adults and children above the age of nine or ten.

The toughest category, either because of duration or steep climbing - or both. Best enjoyed by fit adults and teenagers.

▪ ▪ ▪ ▪ ▪ ▪ ▪ ▪	Path of walk	┢╈╈╈╈╈ Railway line	╱╱╱╱╱ Disused railway line
▭▭▭▭▭▭	Road	△ Hill / tor	
	Lake / reservoir	**N** ⊕ North arrow	
	Urban area	🌳 Woodland	
P	Car park	✝● Church with spire	✝■ Church with tower
◀	Direction arrow	☐ Building	
⌒	Footbridge	◯ Folly / monument etc	

Ingbirchworth Reservoir 1

GETTING THERE: Off the A629 Penistone Huddersfield Road

A pleasant, easy ramble around one of our local reservoirs which provides a safe haven for wildlife. Pick a nice warm day as this is a high, exposed area. It isn't much fun picnicking in a gale. Don't forget the binoculars!

2 miles | About 1 hour | Fountain Inn nearby

Fountain Inn or take a picnic | Fountain Inn | **P** Roadside, near the Fountain Inn in Ingbirchworth

MAP Ordnance Survey Pathfinder: number 715, Barnsley and Penistone *SE 217063*

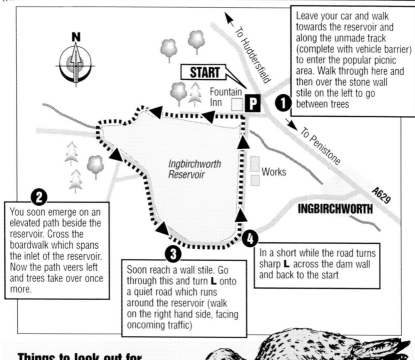

START

To Huddersfield

Fountain Inn **P** **1**

To Penistone

N

Ingbirchworth Reservoir

Works

INGBIRCHWORTH

A629

Leave your car and walk towards the reservoir and along the unmade track (complete with vehicle barrier) to enter the popular picnic area. Walk through here and then over the stone wall stile on the left to go between trees

2 You soon emerge on an elevated path beside the reservoir. Cross the boardwalk which spans the inlet of the reservoir. Now the path veers left and trees take over once more.

3 Soon reach a wall stile. Go through this and turn **L** onto a quiet road which runs around the reservoir (walk on the right hand side, facing oncoming traffic)

4 In a short while the road turns sharp **L** across the dam wall and back to the start

Things to look out for

This reservoir attracts migrating birds and summer breeding species, including Warblers and Swallows. Scan the skies for birds of prey and listen for the burbling call of the Curlew. The latter nest on nearby moors after wintering on our estuaries and are unmistakable with their brown plumage and downcurved bill.

A Curlew

1

2 Cannon Hall

GETTING THERE: Off the A635 road near Cawthorne, Barnsley

This is a nice easy walk with just one climb and clear paths. It can be tackled in any weather, but wellies rather than boots are a good idea after heavy rain.

 4 miles  About 2 hours At Cannon Hall visitor centre

 Cannon Hall   Cherry Tree at High Hoyland **P** At Cannon Hall car park

 **MAP** Ordnance Survey Pathfinder: number 715, Barnsley and Penistone *SE 272079*

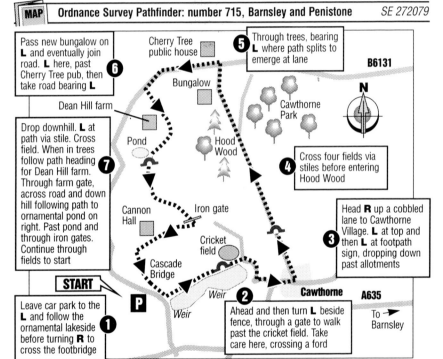

Cherry Tree public house

Bungalow

Dean Hill farm

6 Pass new bungalow on **L** and eventually join road. **L** here, past Cherry Tree pub, then take road bearing **L**

5 Through trees, bearing **L** where path splits to emerge at lane

B6131

N

Cawthorne Park

7 Drop downhill. **L** at path via stile. Cross field. When in trees follow path heading for Dean Hill farm. Through farm gate, across road and down hill following path to ornamental pond on right. Past pond and through iron gates. Continue through fields to start

Pond

Hood Wood

Cannon Hall

Iron gate

4 Cross four fields via stiles before entering Hood Wood

3 Head **R** up a cobbled lane to Cawthorne Village. **L** at top and then **L** at footpath sign, dropping down past allotments

Cricket field

Cascade Bridge

START

P

Weir

Weir

2 Ahead and then turn **L** beside fence, through a gate to walk past the cricket field. Take care here, crossing a ford

Cawthorne A635

To → Barnsley

1 Leave car park to the **L** and follow the ornamental lakeside before turning **R** to cross the footbridge

Things to look out for

This is a lovely area and proof if ever it was needed that Barnsley can compete in landscape terms with its more touristy neighbours.

Cannon Hall is the jewel in the midst of this walk and offers a fine museum and excellent children's farm. Built in the late 18th Century the Hall has fine formal gardens.

Cannon Hall

2

Penistone Circuit 3

Walking is easy around this Pennine market town and although there is some road walking, grass verges are wide and traffic infrequent.

5 miles	3 hours	Penistone town centre

Penistone town centre	Cubley Hall	**P** Penistone town centre

MAP | Ordnance Survey Pathfinder: number 715, Barnsley and Penistone | *SE 247034*

Uphill to road then **R** for 400yds. **L** on clear path which zig-zags between fields **3**

THURLSTONE

Turn **R** on bridleway opposite Brockholes Lane. After 200yds turn **L** on path downhill and past Sike House farm **2**

PENISTONE **P** START

Sike House Farm

Bella Vista Farm

1
Walk up road away from town centre towards Cubley. After half a mile turn **R** up Chapel Lane.

Cubley Hall

4
Path passes near Bella Vista Farm and follows farm lane back to road. **R** here then **L** at next junction

N

6
Half way along track climb stile on **R** to join a footpath which crosses three fields to another quiet road. **R** again to T-junction then **L** to pass Cubley Hall and follow road back to start

5
Follow road for more than a mile. Passing Doubting Farm on **R**, then turn **L** at wide track

Things to look out for

Before your walk take a few minutes to admire the St John the Baptist Parish Church with its superbly carved medieval roof bosses.
Entering the town provides fine views of the many arched railway viaduct built in 1885 and still providing a link between Huddersfield and Sheffield. But for how much longer?

Cubley Hall

4 Little Don

A demanding but rewarding trek to the source of the Little Don, in an area of stunning moorland beauty. Do not attempt this in mist and take both map and compass.

5 miles	allow a good 3 hours	None in area

Take a picnic	Dog and Partridge half way around walk	Yorkshire Water car park on right hand side of A616 north

 MAP **Ordnance Survey Outdoor Leisure: Dark Peak** *SE 202011*

8 It rejoins road at Dog and Partridge, pass this and soon after turn R down track which turns L to become Swinden Lane. Follow back to start

1 Leaving car park go **L** and cross road, walking down to bridleway on **R**. Along track, through woodland to emerge in a clearing

7 Path leaves the stream into higher ground, emerging on A628. Cross to join broad moorland track and follow eastwards

To Holmfirth

 Flouch Inn

START

A628

Snow Road (track)

A628

To Manchester

N

Swinden Lane (track)

To Sheffield

A616

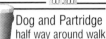 Dog and Partridge

4 The path drops to river level. Follow river, keeping it on left. The path rises again, then drops down. After half a mile, pass elaborate sheep dip on **R**

2 Bear **R** here to cross stream on stepping stones (if you get to a stone bridge you have gone too far) and down beside plantation

3 Go **R** at bottom on path which rises above the Little Don

Sheep fold

Sheep dip

6 When the river splits, take **R** fork north

5 Keep close to river. Walk past wooden footbridge on **L** and stone sheep fold

Things to look out for

In Spring and Summer the Little Don Valley abounds with all sorts of wildlife. Look out for Mountain Hares and Cuckoos which seem attracted there by its seclusion.

Half way along the valley is one of the most elaborate sheep dip complexes in the region, testimony to the wealth wool once generated.

Langsett Moors 5

A bracing trip around one of South Yorkshire's most scenic reservoirs, through pine forests and wild moors. Good underfoot but boots recommended. Avoid it in mist

4 miles 2 hours In car park at National Park Visitor Centre

Cafe across road from start Waggon & Horses nearby **P** Public car park on A616, at Langsett Reservoir

MAP Ordnance Survey Pathfinder number 715: Barnsley and Penistone *SE 211005*

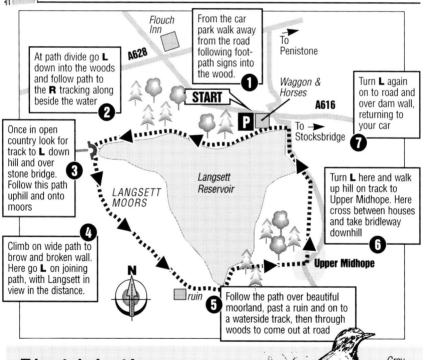

Flouch Inn

A628

From the car park walk away from the road following footpath signs into the wood. **1**

To Penistone

Waggon & Horses

START

A616

To ➤ Stocksbridge

At path divide go **L** down into the woods and follow path to the **R** tracking along beside the water **2**

Turn **L** again on to road and over dam wall, returning to your car **7**

Once in open country look for track to **L** down hill and over stone bridge. Follow this path uphill and onto moors **3**

Langsett Reservoir

LANGSETT MOORS

Turn **L** here and walk up hill on track to Upper Midhope. Here cross between houses and take bridleway downhill **6**

Climb on wide path to brow and broken wall. Here go **L** on joining path, with Langsett in view in the distance. **4**

N

Upper Midhope

ruin **5**

Follow the path over beautiful moorland, past a ruin and on to a waterside track, then through woods to come out at road

Things to look out for

Like so many man-made reservoirs, Langsett is very deep in most sections but the inlet and outlet do harbour birdlife, particularly wildfowl. Take a close look at the weir where the Little Don flows in for Grey Wagtails - which are confusingly rather yellow! - as they grab aquatic larvae in the summer months.

Grey Wagtail

6 Wentworth Castle

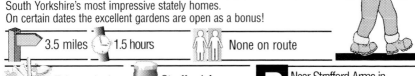

GETTING THERE: M1 North Junct.37, A628 to Dodworth, B6069 to Stainborough

This is an easy Sunday afternoon stroll taking in the grounds of one of South Yorkshire's most impressive stately homes.
On certain dates the excellent gardens are open as a bonus!

3.5 miles | 1.5 hours | None on route

Take a picnic | Strafford Arms | **P** Near Strafford Arms in Stainborough, near Barnsley

MAP | Ordnance Survey Outdoor Pathfinder: number 715, Barnsley & Penistone *SE 326037*

There are several paths about but tend downhill and soon enter open country with a disued railway line on **R**. Then begin to bear **L** again to cross some old workings on a footbridge.

❷

DODWORTH

BARNSLEY

From track beside pub return to main road and turn **L**. Follow it to a footpath along drive on **R**. Follow this as it bears **L** past a house and tracks to **R** of Lowe Wood

Disused railway line

River Dove

❶

N

START

P

Strafford Arms

In front of main house turn **L** and follow footpath down a drive then across fields, **❺** over a footbridge and back on track leading to start

LOWE WOOD

Wentworth Castle

Stainborough Castle

❹

To Sheffield

M1
BIRDWELL

Carry on this clear path uphill to road and go **L**- opposite are the old earthworks of Stainborough Castle. Walk briefly down road then take **❸** path signed on **L** into Lowe Wood once more

Follow clear path then turn **R** where another joins it to return to the road. Cross it and go **L** then **R** up the drive to Wentworth Castle.

Obelisk

△

Steeple Lodge

Things to look out for

The main wing of Wentworth Castle was begun in the 1670s, while the remainder was added in the following century.
The Wentworth dynasty dominated this region for centuries, this section of the family were the Earls of Strafford.
By the road is the unusual Steeple Lodge, now a private house.

Wentworth & Elsecar 7

GETTING THERE: Leave M1 at junction 36 & follow signs for Elsecar

A long but easy walk over undulating country beginning at a relic of our industrial past, taking in one of our finest stately homes and passing three famous follies. Crosses a number of fields so pick a dry or frosty day

8 miles

4 hours *more to enjoy the history*

Wentworth

Plenty in Elsecar and Wentworth

Plenty in Elsecar and Wentworth

P Free at Elsecar Heritage Centre near Barnsley

MAP Ordnance Survey Pathfinder, numbers 726 / 727

SK 388981

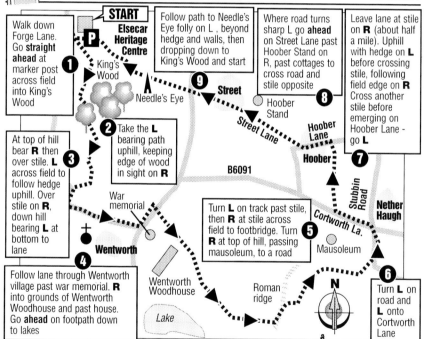

START — **Elsecar Heritage Centre**

1 Walk down Forge Lane. Go **straight ahead** at marker post across field into King's Wood

King's Wood

Follow path to Needle's Eye folly on L , beyond hedge and walls, then dropping down to King's Wood and start

9 Needle's Eye — **Street**

Where road turns sharp L go **ahead** on Street Lane past Hoober Stand on R, past cottages to cross road and stile opposite **8**

Leave lane at stile on **R** (about half a mile). Uphill with hedge on **L** before crossing stile, following field edge on **R** Cross another stile before emerging on Hoober Lane - go **L**

2 Take the **L** bearing path uphill, keeping edge of wood in sight on **R**

Hoober Stand

Street Lane

Hoober Lane

Hoober

7

3 At top of hill bear **R** then over stile. **L** across field to follow hedge uphill. Over stile on **R**, down hill bearing **L** at bottom to lane

War memorial

B6091

Stubbin Road

Nether Haugh

5 Turn **L** on track past stile, then **R** at stile across field to footbridge. Turn **R** at top of hill, passing mausoleum, to a road

Cortworth La.

Mausoleum

4 Follow lane through Wentworth village past war memorial. **R** into grounds of Wentworth Woodhouse and past house. Go **ahead** on footpath down to lakes

Wentworth

Wentworth Woodhouse

Roman ridge

Lake

N

6 Turn **L** on road and **L** onto Cortworth Lane

Things to look out for

Wentworth Woodhouse is arguably one of the most impressive eighteenth century houses in the country - it certainly has the longest frontage. After many years as a college it is now in private ownership, but one can imagine the wealth of its former owners - even the stable block is on a grand scale. A series of follies complete the picture.

8 Scenic Bolsterstone

GETTING THERE: A616 from Sheffield, towards Stocksbridge then Ewden Village

This is a very easy outing, suitable for any weather and especially attractive when snow covers the undulating land of the Ewden Valley.

 4.5 miles 2.5 hours Bolsterstone

Bolsterstone, or take a picnic	The Castle, Bolsterstone	**P**	In Bolsterstone, considerately, near church

MAP Ordnance Survey Pathfinder: number 726, Sheffield (North) *SK 271968*

STOCKSBRIDGE

N

Follow clear path, along ridge. After about half a mile, pass Cote House and continue on footpath to reach a clear track. **R** here and down to road
2

Leave village passing church on **R** and school on **L**. Immediately after, hard **L** and over stile
1

To Stocksbridge

START

P **BOLSTERSTONE**

Cote House

L at road, passing More Hall on **R**. Just before road turn **R** and dogleg on to lower, quiet road back to Reservoir
3

EWDEN VILLAGE

More Hall

A6102

More Hall Reservoir

Pass reservoir and at Ewden Village, uphill on minor road back to Bolsterstone. Half way up hill, take footpath on **R** to cross two fields back to village
4

Things to look out for

Like so many other valleys around Sheffield, Ewden has its reservoirs, in this case More Hall and Broomhead.
Ewden village once housed the dam builders but now is the only real accommodation in the valley. On the hill above, complete with church and pub is Bolsterstone, famous for its championship winning male voice choir.

The Bradfields & Agden 9

This walk takes in the twin villages of High & Low Bradfield west of Sheffield. A fine introduction to an area dotted with reservoirs set amid typical peat moorland. The trek can be tackled safely in all but the harshest conditions

5 miles	2.5 hours		Low Bradfield
Take a picnic	The Plough Inn The Old Horns Inn	**P**	Park in the village of Low Bradfield

MAP | Ordnance Survey Pathfinder: number 726 Sheffield (North) & Stocksbridge *SK 264918*

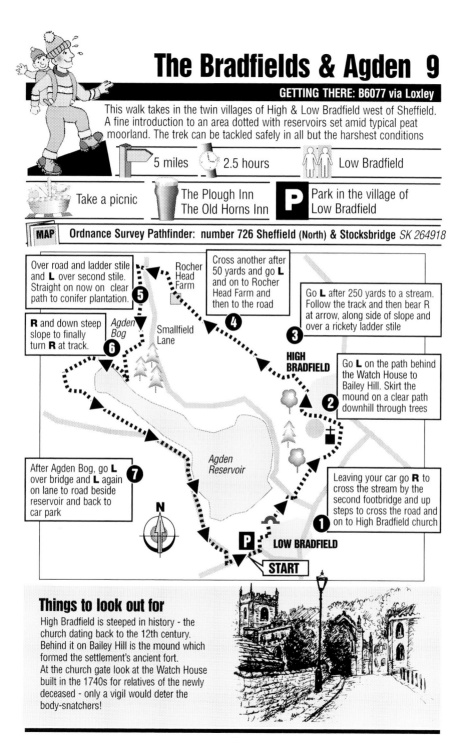

Over road and ladder stile and **L** over second stile. Straight on now on clear path to conifer plantation.
5

Rocher Head Farm

Cross another after 50 yards and go **L** and on to Rocher Head Farm and then to the road
4

Go **L** after 250 yards to a stream. Follow the track and then bear R at arrow, along side of slope and over a rickety ladder stile
3

R and down steep slope to finally turn **R** at track.
6

Agden Bog

Smallfield Lane

HIGH BRADFIELD

Go **L** on the path behind the Watch House to Bailey Hill. Skirt the mound on a clear path downhill through trees
2

After Agden Bog, go **L** over bridge and **L** again on lane to road beside reservoir and back to car park
7

Agden Reservoir

Leaving your car go **R** to cross the stream by the second footbridge and up steps to cross the road and on to High Bradfield church
1

N

P **LOW BRADFIELD**

START

Things to look out for

High Bradfield is steeped in history - the church dating back to the 12th century. Behind it on Bailey Hill is the mound which formed the settlement's ancient fort. At the church gate look at the Watch House built in the 1740s for relatives of the newly deceased - only a vigil would deter the body-snatchers!

9

10 Grenoside Woods

GETTING THERE: A61 out of Sheffield, village uphill on left

This is a lovely wander, almost entirely along woodland tracks and bridleways which, although known by locals, are little explored.

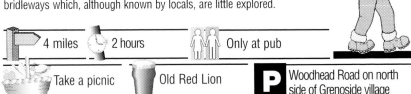

4 miles   2 hours   Only at pub

Take a picnic   Old Red Lion   **P** Woodhead Road on north side of Grenoside village

MAP Ordnance Survey Pathfinder: number 726, Sheffield (North)   *SK 327947*

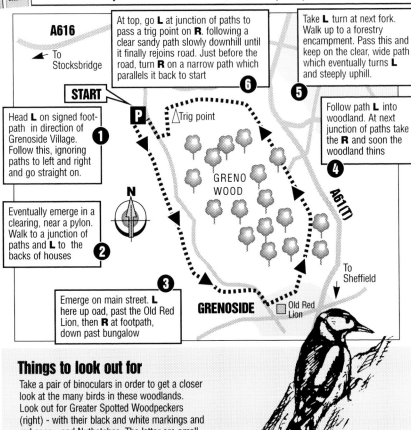

A616

← To Stocksbridge

At top, go **L** at junction of paths to pass a trig point on **R**. following a clear sandy path slowly downhill until it finally rejoins road. Just before the road, turn **R** on a narrow path which parallels it back to start **6**

Take **L** turn at next fork. Walk up to a forestry encampment. Pass this and keep on the clear, wide path which eventually turns **L** and steeply uphill. **5**

START

△Trig point

1 Head **L** on signed footpath in direction of Grenoside Village. Follow this, ignoring paths to left and right and go straight on.

Follow path **L** into woodland. At next junction of paths take the **R** and soon the woodland thins **4**

GRENO WOOD

N

A61(T)

2 Eventually emerge in a clearing, near a pylon. Walk to a junction of paths and **L** to the backs of houses

To Sheffield

3 Emerge on main street. **L** here up oad, past the Old Red Lion, then **R** at footpath, down past bungalow

GRENOSIDE   ▢ Old Red Lion

Things to look out for

Take a pair of binoculars in order to get a closer look at the many birds in these woodlands. Look out for Greater Spotted Woodpeckers (right) - with their black and white markings and red caps - and Nuthatches. The latter are small blue and buff birds which nest in holes in trees. If the holes are too big, they simply paste them up with mud!

10

Howden Edge 11

This is a hard walk in true Dark Peak country. Rare amongst this collection it is not recommended for children.
Make sure you know how to use a map and compass.

6 miles	4 hours	None on route
Take a picnic	None on route	**P** Fairholmes (catch bus to Kings Tree on Summer weekends)

MAP Ordnance Survey Outdoor Leisure: The Dark Peak   *SK 169951*

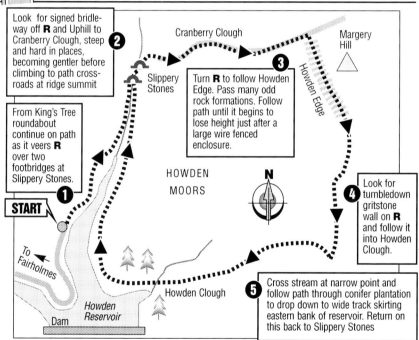

Look for signed bridleway off **R** and Uphill to Cranberry Clough, steep and hard in places, becoming gentler before climbing to path crossroads at ridge summit **2**

From King's Tree roundabout continue on path as it veers **R** over two footbridges at Slippery Stones. **1**

START

Cranberry Clough

Margery Hill

Slippery Stones

Turn **R** to follow Howden Edge. Pass many odd rock formations. Follow path until it begins to lose height just after a large wire fenced enclosure. **3**

Howden Edge

HOWDEN MOORS

N

Look for tumbledown gritstone wall on **R** and follow it into Howden Clough. **4**

To Fairholmes

Howden Clough

Cross stream at narrow point and follow path through conifer plantation to drop down to wide track skirting eastern bank of reservoir. Return on this back to Slippery Stones **5**

Howden Reservoir

Dam

Things to look out for

The long ridge known further south as Derwent Edge and here as Howden Edge is notable not only for its views. The winds and rains of time have worn and fashioned the gritstone exposed at the surface into all sorts of shapes. Considering the surreal nature of some of their names, one wonders what our ancestors had in their hip flasks!

Slippery Stones

12 Bradfield Moors

GETTING THERE: A57 from Sheffield, right to pass Strines pub

A long walk, not be attempted with small children.
A dry, clear day is recommmended, together with the skill to use a map and compass. This is exceptional wilderness walking.

 10 miles | At least 5 hours make a day of it | None on route

Take a picnic | Strines Inn | **P** Car park on left downhill from Strines Pub

MAP Ordnance Survey Pathfinder No 726, Sheffield North *SK 221909*

2 R and follow the path to the right of prominent Back Tor and follow a clear ridge of rising ground.

 Back Tor

3 Soon reach a collection of prominent rocks. Pass these and then follow the path as it wends **R** to eventually join Dukes Road - a wider path - heading east and slowly downhill

Walk uphill away from road on broad, track.. This is Foulstone Drive which continues uphill to finally reach a crossroad of paths on Derwent Edge. The views ahead are magnificent.

Foulstone Drive

1 **START**

Hallfield House

Dale Dike Reservoir

Derwent Edge

P

Strines Pub   To A57

Strines Reservoir

N

4 At road, turn **R**. Follow it for about 1.5 miles. Ignore road **L**, but soon take bridleway on **L** downhill to minor road above Dale Dike Reservoir.

5 R here on road then follow it **R** and then ahead to Thompson House. Take bridleway and path, passing Hallfield House and then reach the house at Brogging. Here take the track **R** of the house and uphill to road. **L** here back to carpark

Things to look out for

One of Britain's rarest birds of prey, the Goshawk, still has an outpost in the Peak District, although it is still ruthlessly persecuted by gamekeepers who see it as a threat to grouse. Goshawks like to nest in pine forests and can sometimes be seen flying above the moors of the Dark Peak which has plenty of such woodland.

Dale Dike Circuit 13

GETTING THERE: A57 Glossop road from Sheffield, and leave it at sign for Strines Inn

An easy, all weather walk in a picturesque valley. The route is well sign-posted throughout with the child-friendly Strines pub just half a mile away.

Just over 3 miles	2.5 hours	Strines Inn
Strines Inn	Strines Inn	**P** On Mortimer Rd, (known as Strines Rd), near 'Brogging' track

MAP Ordnance Survey Pathfinder: number 726 Sheffield (North) & Stocksbridge *SK 228908*

6 Follow this clear path past Hallfield and Stubbing Farm and return to Brogging

5 Bear **L** up track through pine woods to road **L** here and up, past farm track on left and on to bridleway, (**L**)

4 Turn **L** at sign to water's edge. **R** and on to dam wall, down via steps to cross outlet at footbridge

1 Go down the track to Brogging House and bear **R** down path below wall of Strines Reservoir.

START

P

Mortimer Road

Hallifield Farm

Dale Dike Reservoir

3 Go **L** and follow the yellow path markers across several fields before entering more woods

Strines Bridge

Strines Inn

To A57

Strines Reservoir

2 Over the stile and into trees before crossing footbridge and then wall stile

Andrew Wood

N

Things to look out for

Dale Dike Reservoir, one of a series of four in this valley was built in the 1870's to serve the ever-growing city of Sheffield. Near the outflow look out for marker stones from a previous dam which burst its banks in 1864 sending a tidal-wave down the valley drowning more than 200 people.

Dale Dike Bridge

14 Sheffield & Tinsley Canal

GETTING THERE: From Sheffield City Centre

This ramble along Sheffield's forgotten waterway is on good paths throughout - it was built for barge dragging horses after all - but ensure children keep away from the edge.

 4 miles   2 hours   Sheffield City Centre

Sheffield centre or take a picnic   The Sheaf at Victoria Quays   **P** Sheffield City Centre.

MAP | None needed, but Ordnance Survey Pathfinder: number 743, Sheffield, adds interest

Set off from the marvellously redeveloped Canal Basin and admire the restored warehouses **1**

There follows a succession of bridges, most of the older ones with name plaques. Pass many factories and workshops. **3**

Continue on opposite bank. After a short while reach Tinsley Locks, an amazing example of 19th Century engineering **5**

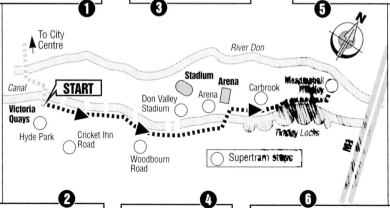

Cross the canal via swing bridge and walk down towpath away from city. (with your back to city the towpath is on **R**) **2**

After a couple of miles, leave towpath on a new path, cross the canal via a new bridge with a good view of Sheffield Arena **4**

Soon after the locks, the canal swings left before going under the M1 motorway. Leave via another new bridge which leads to the Supertram stop to return to start via tram **6**

Things to look out for

Not long ago this canal resembled all the others in the industrial north of England; polluted, rubbish filled and lifeless. Now though it teems with life and on hot days carp, roach and perch can be seen shoaling near the surface. Waterhens abound and look out for the odd flash of electric blue as a kingfisher dashes by.

14

Ulley Country Park 15

GETTING THERE: A618 from Rotherham or leave M1, jcn. 31, & take B6067 via Aston

An easy, attractive and interesting ramble around one of the many reservoirs in South Yorkshire which have been opened to public access. Walking is easy on clear paths at any time of the year. Ideal for families. Remember to take a picnic in warm weather!

Just over 2 miles | 2 hours *more to observe wildlife* | At the park entrance

Take a picnic | Royal Oak at Ulley | **P** Country park, beside A618 (Rotherham/Swallownest road)

MAP Ordnance Survey Pathfinder: number 744, Aughton & Carlton in Lindrick *SK 878453*

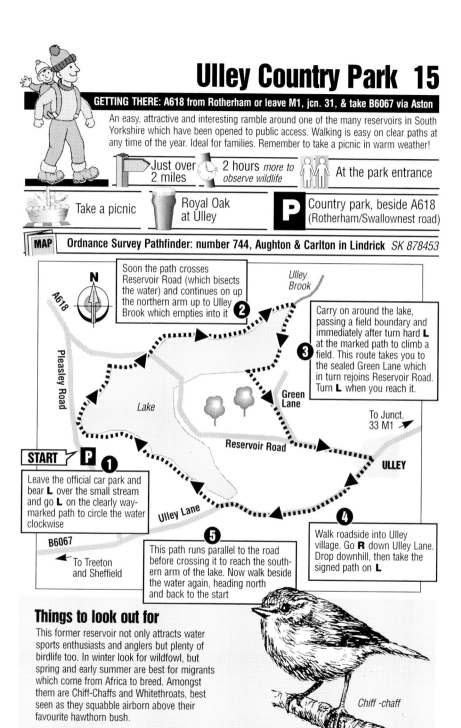

N

A618

Soon the path crosses Reservoir Road (which bisects the water) and continues on up the northern arm up to Ulley Brook which empties into it **2**

Ulley Brook

Carry on around the lake, passing a field boundary and immediately after turn hard **L** at the marked path to climb a field. This route takes you to the sealed Green Lane which in turn rejoins Reservoir Road. Turn **L** when you reach it. **3**

Pleasley Road

Lake

Green Lane

To Junct. 33 M1 ➤

Reservoir Road

START **P** **1**

ULLEY

Leave the official car park and bear **L** over the small stream and go **L** on the clearly way-marked path to circle the water clockwise

Ulley Lane

4

B6067

◄ To Treeton and Sheffield

5
This path runs parallel to the road before crossing it to reach the southern arm of the lake. Now walk beside the water again, heading north and back to the start

Walk roadside into Ulley village. Go **R** down Ulley Lane. Drop downhill, then take the signed path on **L**

Things to look out for

This former reservoir not only attracts water sports enthusiasts and anglers but plenty of birdlife too. In winter look for wildfowl, but spring and early summer are best for migrants which come from Africa to breed. Amongst them are Chiff-Chaffs and Whitethroats, best seen as they squabble airborn above their favourite hawthorn bush.

Chiff -chaff

15

16 Industrial Sheffield

GETTING THERE: Shalesmoor via Supertram

An easy, but fascinating tour around Sheffield's industrial backyard with some interesting buildings. Do it on a gloomy November afternoon for maximum atmosphere. Maybe fit in a vist to Kelham Island Museum on route

| 2 miles | 1 hour | City Centre |

| City Centre | City Centre or Fat Cat near Kelham Island | **P** Car parks in City Centre or use Supertram to Shalesmoor |

MAP A Sheffield A - Z street map is ideal *SK 351883*

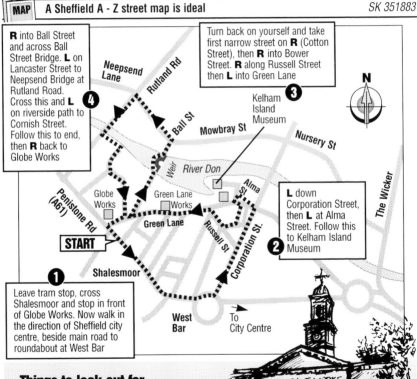

R into Ball Street and across Ball Street Bridge. **L** on Lancaster Street to Neepsend Bridge at Rutland Road. Cross this and **L** on riverside path to Cornish Street. Follow this to end, then **R** back to Globe Works

Turn back on yourself and take first narrow street on **R** (Cotton Street), then **R** into Bower Street. **R** along Russell Street then **L** into Green Lane

L down Corporation Street, then **L** at Alma Street. Follow this to Kelham Island Museum

Leave tram stop, cross Shalesmoor and stop in front of Globe Works. Now walk in the direction of Sheffield city centre, beside main road to roundabout at West Bar

Neepsend Lane · Rutland Rd · Kelham Island Museum · Mowbray St · Nursery St · Ball St · River Don · Weir · Globe Works · Green Lane Works · Green Lane · Penistone Rd (A61) · Russell St · Alma St · Corporation St · The Wicker · START · Shalesmoor · West Bar · To City Centre

Things to look out for

The Globe Works, close to our start point, is believed to be the world's oldest "factory". Built in the eighteenth century it housed a collection of craftsmen working under one elaborate roof and creating famous Sheffield cutlery. At that time, this "manufactory", was in the middle of fields - how times changed in just a few decades! We also pass the elaborate frontage of Green Lane works

The Moss Valley 17

This is an easy stroll for all the family, starting and finishing at a welcoming pub. The Moss Valley, despite its neighbouring suburbs, retains an air of rural tranquility.

3 miles | 2 hours | Opposite Bridge Inn

Bridge Inn or Take a pinic | Bridge Inn, Ford | **P** Public Car Park near to Bridge Inn at Ford

MAP | **Ordnance Survey Pathfinder: number 744, Aughton** | *SK 403805*

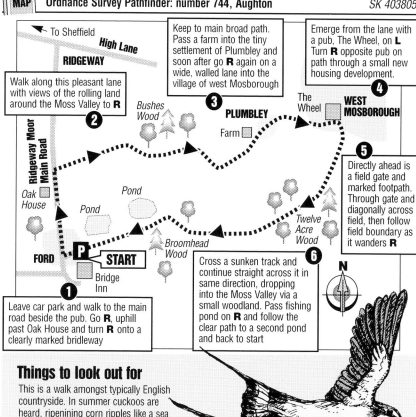

← To Sheffield

High Lane

RIDGEWAY

Walk along this pleasant lane with views of the rolling land around the Moss Valley to **R**
2

Keep to main broad path. Pass a farm into the tiny settlement of Plumbley and soon after go **R** again on a wide, walled lane into the village of west Mosborough
3

Emerge from the lane with a pub, The Wheel, on **L** Turn **R** opposite pub on path through a small new housing development.
4

Bushes Wood

PLUMBLEY

Farm

The Wheel | **WEST MOSBOROUGH**

5

Directly ahead is a field gate and marked footpath. Through gate and diagonally across field, then follow field boundary as it wanders **R**

Ridgeway Moor Main Road

Oak House

Pond

Pond

Pond

Twelve Acre Wood

Broomhead Wood

FORD

P **START**

Bridge Inn

N

Cross a sunken track and continue straight across it in same direction, dropping into the Moss Valley via a small woodland. Pass fishing pond on **R** and follow the clear path to a second pond and back to start
6

Leave car park and walk to the main road beside the pub. Go **R**, uphill past Oak House and turn **R** onto a clearly marked bridleway
1

Things to look out for

This is a walk amongst typically English countryside. In summer cuckoos are heard, ripenining corn ripples like a sea in the breeze and swallows swoop overhead. Near the ponds, the smell of wild garlic fills the air, particularly on a hot day.
There is a pretty picnic site, or if you prefer, the Bridge Inn provides a resting spot.

18 Redmires & Rivelin

An easy stroll over Hallam Moors from Redmires to the Rivelin Valley and back via Wyming Brook. Good views over Sheffield and west to the Peak District.

4 miles	3 hours	None in area

Take a picnic	Sportsman and Three Merry Lads	**P** At Redmires Reservoir at the top of Redmires Road

MAP Ordnance Survey Pathfinder: number 743 Sheffield   *SK 256857*

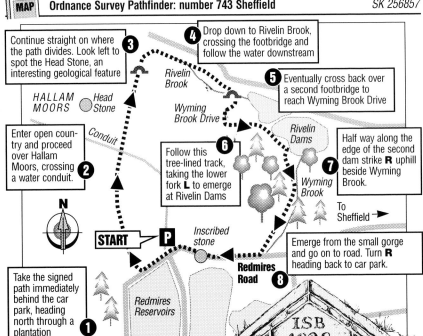

3 Continue straight on where the path divides. Look left to spot the Head Stone, an interesting geological feature

4 Drop down to Rivelin Brook, crossing the footbridge and follow the water downstream

5 Eventually cross back over a second footbridge to reach Wyming Brook Drive

HALLAM MOORS   Head Stone

Rivelin Brook

Wyming Brook Drive

Rivelin Dams

2 Enter open country and proceed over Hallam Moors, crossing a water conduit.

Conduit

6 Follow this tree-lined track, taking the lower fork **L** to emerge at Rivelin Dams

7 Half way along the edge of the second dam strike **R** uphill beside Wyming Brook.

Wyming Brook

To Sheffield →

N

START   **P**

Inscribed stone

Redmires Road

Emerge from the small gorge and go on to road. Turn **R** heading back to car park. **8**

1 Take the signed path immediately behind the car park, heading north through a plantation

Redmires Reservoirs

ISB 1828

ICH DIEN DINNER

Things to look out for

Emerging on the road back to the car park look on the left for a stone inscribed "Ich Dien Dinner" - "I serve dinner" which once stood above the door of an old coaching inn.

Look out in Spring and Summer for Wheatears, small colourful moorland nesters. Wheatear is a genteel form of the old country name "white arse"!

Redmires circuit 19

GETTING THERE: Leaving Sheffield on A57, take Redmires Road

A walk with marvellous views of Sheffield to one side and the Redmires reservoir system to the other. Good paths throughout, if a little soft in places. Don't attempt in misty weather.

5 miles | Allow 3 hours | None on route

Take a picnic | Three Merry Lads & Sportsman | **P** At Redmires

MAP Ordnance Survey Pathfinder: number 743, Sheffield | *SK 256857*

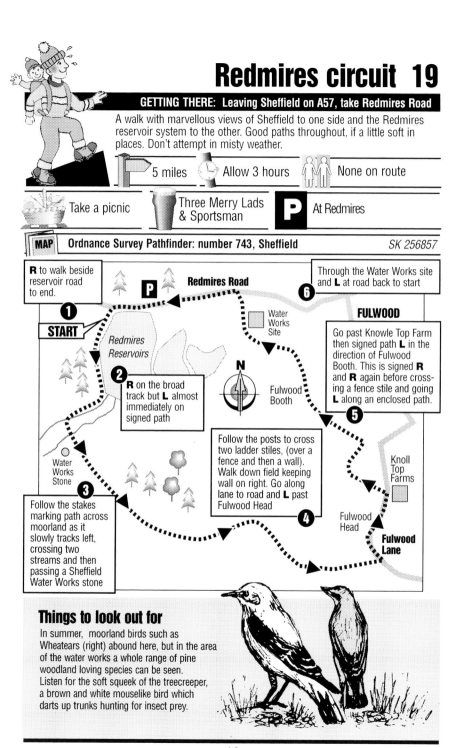

R to walk beside reservoir road to end.

P **Redmires Road**

START ❶

Redmires Reservoirs

❷ **R** on the broad track but **L** almost immediately on signed path

Water Works Stone

❸ Follow the stakes marking path across moorland as it slowly tracks left, crossing two streams and then passing a Sheffield Water Works stone

Water Works Site

N

Fulwood Booth

Follow the posts to cross two ladder stiles, (over a fence and then a wall). Walk down field keeping wall on right. Go along lane to road and **L** past Fulwood Head ❹

Through the Water Works site and **L** at road back to start ❻

FULWOOD

Go past Knowle Top Farm then signed path **L** in the direction of Fulwood Booth. This is signed **R** and **R** again before crossing a fence stile and going **L** along an enclosed path. ❺

Knoll Top Farms

Fulwood Head

Fulwood Lane

Things to look out for

In summer, moorland birds such as Wheatears (right) abound here, but in the area of the water works a whole range of pine woodland loving species can be seen. Listen for the soft squeek of the treecreeper, a brown and white mouselike bird which darts up trunks hunting for insect prey.

20 Mayfield Valley

GETTING THERE: Ecclesall Road then Ringinglow Road

Good in any weather, this walk can be enjoyed year round.
The streamside section will be particularly popular with children.

3 miles	2 hours	None on route

Norfolk Arms or take a picnic	Norfolk Arms	**P** Opposite Norfolk Arms

MAP Ordnance Survey Pathfinder: number 743, Sheffield   *SK 291838*

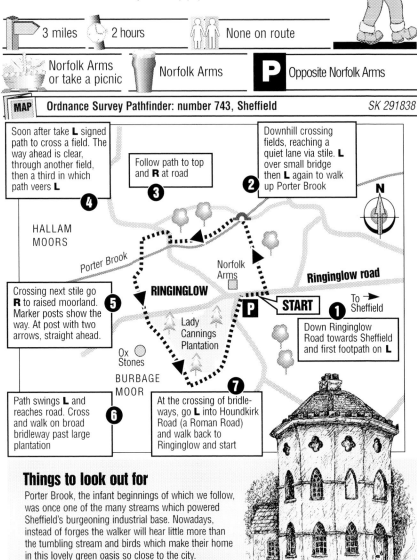

4 Soon after take **L** signed path to cross a field. The way ahead is clear, through another field, then a third in which path veers **L**

3 Follow path to top and **R** at road

2 Downhill crossing fields, reaching a quiet lane via stile. **L** over small bridge then **L** again to walk up Porter Brook

HALLAM MOORS

Porter Brook

N

Norfolk Arms

Ringinglow road

RINGINGLOW

5 Crossing next stile go **R** to raised moorland. Marker posts show the way. At post with two arrows, straight ahead.

P

START

1

To → Sheffield

Lady Cannings Plantation

1 Down Ringinglow Road towards Sheffield and first footpath on **L**

Ox Stones

BURBAGE MOOR

6 Path swings **L** and reaches road. Cross and walk on broad bridleway past large plantation

7 At the crossing of bridle-ways, go **L** into Houndkirk Road (a Roman Road) and walk back to Ringinglow and start

Things to look out for

Porter Brook, the infant beginnings of which we follow, was once one of the many streams which powered Sheffield's burgeoning industrial base. Nowadays, instead of forges the walker will hear little more than the tumbling stream and birds which make their home in this lovely green oasis so close to the city.
The unusual Round House (right), an old toll house for Houndkirk Road, is opposite the Norfolk Arms.

Seal Stones 21

This is a much tougher walk than usual, particularly on the early section, however, the views make it worth the effort.
Avoid it in mist and don't try tackling it with children.

5 miles

3 hours
to enjoy views

Nearest at Snake Inn

Only at pub
(take supplies)

Snake Pass Inn

P Small lay-by on A 57 on
Sheffield side of Snake Inn

MAP Ordnance Survey Outdoor Leisure: The Dark Peak

SK 113906

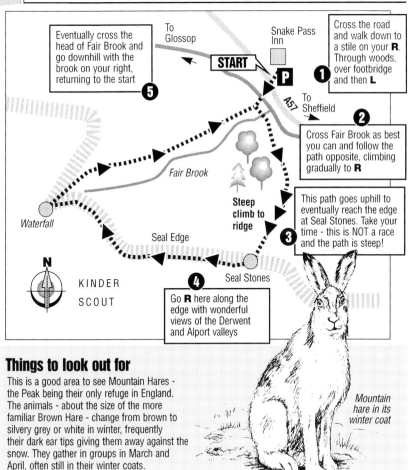

Eventually cross the head of Fair Brook and go downhill with the brook on your right, returning to the start **5**

To Glossop

Snake Pass Inn

START

Cross the road and walk down to a stile on your **R**. Through woods, over footbridge and then **L** **1**

To Sheffield

2 Cross Fair Brook as best you can and follow the path opposite, climbing gradually to **R**

Fair Brook

Steep climb to ridge

This path goes uphill to eventually reach the edge at Seal Stones. Take your time - this is NOT a race and the path is steep! **3**

Waterfall

Seal Edge

N

KINDER

SCOUT

4 Seal Stones

Go **R** here along the edge with wonderful views of the Derwent and Alport valleys

Things to look out for

This is a good area to see Mountain Hares - the Peak being their only refuge in England. The animals - about the size of the more familiar Brown Hare - change from brown to silvery grey or white in winter, frequently their dark ear tips giving them away against the snow. They gather in groups in March and April, often still in their winter coats.

Mountain hare in its winter coat

21

22 Alport Castles

GETTING THERE: A57 Sheffield to Manchester Road (Snake Pass)

A long but rewarding walk along a hidden Dark Peak valley followed by a moorland trek. The area is under threat from disturbance by logging operations in nearby plantations.

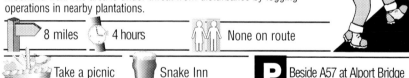

8 miles	4 hours		None on route

Take a picnic	Snake Inn	**P**	Beside A57 at Alport Bridge

MAP   **Ordnance Survey Outdoor Leisure: The Dark Peak**   *SK 141895*

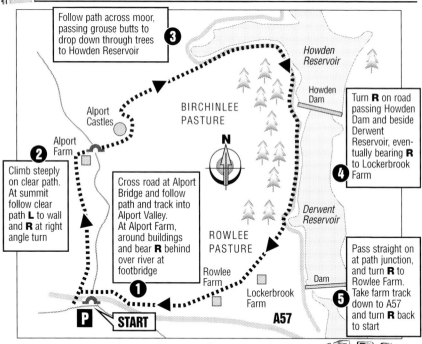

3 Follow path across moor, passing grouse butts to drop down through trees to Howden Reservoir

Howden Reservoir

Howden Dam

4 Turn **R** on road passing Howden Dam and beside Derwent Reservoir, eventually bearing **R** to Lockerbrook Farm

BIRCHINLEE PASTURE

Alport Castles

Alport Farm

2 Climb steeply on clear path. At summit follow clear path **L** to wall and **R** at right angle turn

1 Cross road at Alport Bridge and follow path and track into Alport Valley. At Alport Farm, around buildings and bear **R** behind over river at footbridge

Derwent Reservoir

ROWLEE PASTURE

Rowlee Farm

Lockerbrook Farm

Dam

5 Pass straight on at path junction, and turn **R** to Rowlee Farm. Take farm track down to A57 and turn **R** back to start

A57

P **START**

Things to look out for

The Alport Valley must be one of the most picturesque in the Dark Peak and is dominated on its eastern flank by the largest landslip in Britain.
Our walk tracks beside this and passes the "castles" themselves, large towers of millstone grit which have literally fallen away from the ridge.

Howden Dam

Derwent Edge 23

This is an easy walk to the Dark Peak's longest edge with wonderful views towards Kinder and the Hope Valley. Paths are clear and well marked, but avoid the Edge in mist.

4 miles   2 hours   Ladybower Inn

Ladybower Inn *passed on way back*   Ladybower Inn   **P** Lay-by beside A57 Sheffield/Manchester Road

MAP Ordnance Survey Pathfinder: Sheffield 743 & Outdoor Leisure: Dark Peak *SK 214875*

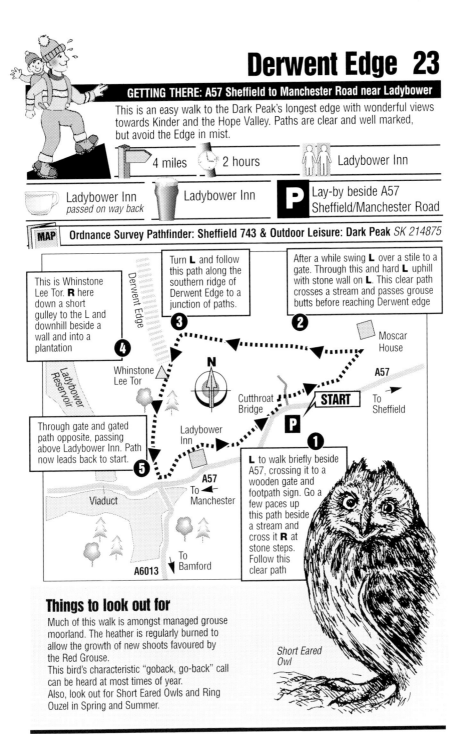

Derwent Edge

This is Whinstone Lee Tor. **R** here down a short gulley to the L and downhill beside a wall and into a plantation **④**

Turn **L** and follow this path along the southern ridge of Derwent Edge to a junction of paths. **③**

After a while swing **L** over a stile to a gate. Through this and hard **L** uphill with stone wall on **L**. This clear path crosses a stream and passes grouse butts before reaching Derwent edge **②**

Moscar House

Whinstone Lee Tor

Ladybower Reservoir

N

Cutthroat Bridge

START

A57

To Sheffield

Through gate and gated path opposite, passing above Ladybower Inn. Path now leads back to start. **⑤**

Ladybower Inn

P

①

A57 To Manchester

Viaduct

To Bamford

A6013

L to walk briefly beside A57, crossing it to a wooden gate and footpath sign. Go a few paces up this path beside a stream and cross it **R** at stone steps. Follow this clear path

Things to look out for

Much of this walk is amongst managed grouse moorland. The heather is regularly burned to allow the growth of new shoots favoured by the Red Grouse.
This bird's characteristic "goback, go-back" call can be heard at most times of year.
Also, look out for Short Eared Owls and Ring Ouzel in Spring and Summer.

Short Eared Owl

24 Above Ladybower

GETTING THERE: Take A57 from Sheffield towards Manchester

Although a reasonable height is gained on this walk it is relatively easy with terrific views rewarding a little temporary breathlessness. Best avoided in mist.

 4 miles   2 hours   None on route

 Take a picnic   Ladybower Inn   **P** Lay by, Sheffield side of viaduct, or large public car park just after

MAP   Ordnance Survey Outdoor Leisure: The Dark Peak   *SK 195864*

At top turn hard **L** on signed bridleway. After half a mile path veers **L** and drops down-hill to reach three ancient farm buildings. Through small gate near barn and downhill to wide path beside reservoir and **L** back to start

Old farm buildings

2 Follow path, slowly climbing uphill. Soon after the only real climb is encountered, in a narrow gully, but the toil is short lived

3

N

To Manchester

Cottages

Viaduct

P

A57

P   **START**   A57   To Sheffield

Ladybower Reservoir

Cross A57. Walk up metalled track opposite, past cottages. Soon after go **L** at footpath sign **1** via a gate into woodland.

Things to look out for

In the years before and after the last war, vast tracts of land in the Derwent Valley were planted with pine trees. Although of use to man they are little if any to beasts with birds ignoring them and plantlife unable to survive

Happily, many are now being thinned and replaced by natural, broadleafed species of value to birds and insects.

24

Ughill Moor & Strines 25

This is an easy and rewarding walk taking in high moors and a quiet section beside one of our many reservoirs. Sugworth House has a fine show of snowdrops in early Spring.

 5 miles   3 hours Strines Inn

Strines Inn Strines Inn **P** Halfway up hill, track on left

 MAP Ordnance Survey Pathfinder: 726 Sheffield (North), and 743 Sheffield *SK 240883*

From here drop down towards Dale Dike Reservoir and head **R** on the clear path through fields

Dale Dike Reservoir

❸

Once in Andrew Wood follow the footpath sign **R** and walk uphill, crossing two quiet roads before going through a second wood

❹

Andrew Wood

Strines Inn

Strines Reservoir

Folly

N

Sugworth Hall

Ughill Moors

Sugworth Road

❺ Take a **R** turn on emerging and then **L** along Snake Hill Road; this is a clear bridlepath which takes you back to your start point

Snake Hill Road

❷

Turn **R** at the footpath sign and follow the wall to Sugworth Road and go **R** down drive of Sugworth House (right of way) and along the path to the **R** of the house and on to Boot's Folly

Follow the track away from road, above Moscar Heights, through two gates

❶

START **P**

Hollow Meadows To Sheffield →

A57

Things to look out for

Although not directly on the route the Strines Inn is likely to feature in this day out - dating from the end of the 13th Century its windows offer grand views of our route.

Look out on the way for Short Eared Owls. These ground-nesting birds hunt in daylight and are a common sight in spring and summer as they drift along.

26 Ladybower

An enjoyable and straightforward walk on clear paths with very good views across the reservoir and Derwent Edge beyond. One for a day when mist covers the higher tops.

 4 miles   2 hours   Near start of walk

 Take a picnic   Yorkshire Bridge/ Ladybower Inn   **P** Free Severn Trent car park at Heathdene on A6013

MAP Ordnance Survey Outdoor Leisure: The Dark Peak   *SK 203853*

This path now wends its way downhill, turning **R** to join a lower path beside the reservoir. Follow this **R** to regain the outward route and retrace your steps **6**

To Glossop

A57

N

To Sheffield   **A57**

Walk **L** through the car park on a signed path above the main road and then drop down to a memorial to the Derwent dam builders via steps **1**

Ladybower Reservoir   Viaduct   **START**   **P**

Cross a stile and then go **L** on the grassy path and onwards to cross a second stile. The views across the reservoir are stunning **5**

Toilets
Yorkshire Bridge Inn

2

Go **L** now and then over a stile for a brief stride uphill to the track of a former railway line **R** on this to the dam wall, then just past it to veer **L** and uphill **4**

Follow this path amongst scattered woodland - listening to the songbirds as you go and just before the steel gate veer **R** down to a stile and cross Yorkshire Bridge **3**

Cross the road (take care it can be busy) and then **L** again to a dam wall. Just before the public toilets go **R** at a gap in the wall. Drop downhill on a good path **2**

Things to look out for

Ladybower Reservoir was the third in the Derwent series to be completed, only officially opened at the end of the last war. Although too deep to attract much birdlife the land at its edges attracts breeding migrants; happily, work is under way to remove the pine plantations of the past and replace them with broadleaf woodland.

Kinder from the South 27

This is a hard walk along one of Kinder's most important valleys. Compass, map and ability to use both is essential. Not advisable for young children.

6 miles   3 hours   Nearest at Edale

Take a picnic   In the village of Edale   **P** Car park at Edale

MAP   Ordnance Survey Outdoor Leisure: The Dark Peak   *SK 124853*

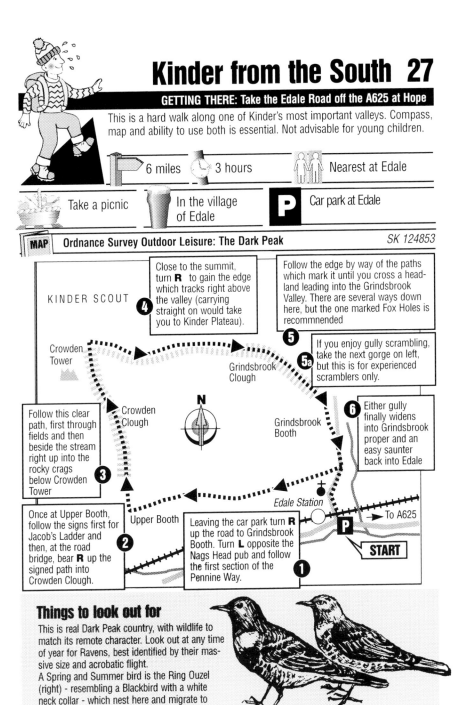

KINDER SCOUT

4 Close to the summit, turn **R** to gain the edge which tracks right above the valley (carrying straight on would take you to Kinder Plateau).

5 Follow the edge by way of the paths which mark it until you cross a headland leading into the Grindsbrook Valley. There are several ways down here, but the one marked Fox Holes is recommnended

Crowden Tower

Grindsbrook Clough

5a If you enjoy gully scrambling, take the next gorge on left, but this is for experienced scramblers only.

Crowden Clough

Grindsbrook Booth

6 Either gully finally widens into Grindsbrook proper and an easy saunter back into Edale

3 Follow this clear path, first through fields and then beside the stream right up into the rocky crags below Crowden Tower

Edale Station

To A625

2 Once at Upper Booth, follow the signs first for Jacob's Ladder and then, at the road bridge, bear **R** up the signed path into Crowden Clough.

Upper Booth

1 Leaving the car park turn **R** up the road to Grindsbrook Booth. Turn **L** opposite the Nags Head pub and follow the first section of the Pennine Way.

P

START

Things to look out for

This is real Dark Peak country, with wildlife to match its remote character. Look out at any time of year for Ravens, best identified by their massive size and acrobatic flight.
A Spring and Summer bird is the Ring Ouzel (right) - resembling a Blackbird with a white neck collar - which nest here and migrate to Africa in the autumn.

28 Kinder Edge Walk

GETTING THERE: Take the Edale Valley Road from Hope, off the A625 to Castleton

A hard walk on rough ground, but with rewarding views into the Edale Valley. Only attempt this walk in good, clear weather and ensure you can use map and compass.

 5 miles   4 hours   Edale

Edale, or take a picnic   Edale   **P** National Park car park at Edale, (fee)

MAP Ordnance Survey Outdoor Leisure: The Dark Peak   *SK 124853*

At summit, turn **R**. and follow edge on rocky path
3

This skirting route takes in the rising Upper Tor and then Nether Tor before arriving at Ringing Roger
4

Nether Tor   Ringing Roger

Upper Tor

KINDER PLATEAU

Grindsbrook Clough

Grinds Brook

The interesting descent is a little further on via Ollerbrook Clough, on a clear path to Ollerbrook Booth. **R** here for easy walk back to Edale
5

Soon path bears up and **L**, narrowing into sheltered ravine of Grindsbrook Clough.
2

N

Grindsbrook Booth

Ollerbrook Booth

EDALE

Up road from Edale to Grindsbrook Booth. Once road becomes a track, follow clear path **R** over footbridge and begin ascending Grinds Brook
1

START

P

Things to look out for

Ravens are now largely confined to the Lake District and highland Scotland. Nonetheless, the odd bird does turn up in the Peak District. Huge and black - although there is rarely a crow at hand with which to compare them - their swooping closed wing dives and raucous cawing call gives them away.

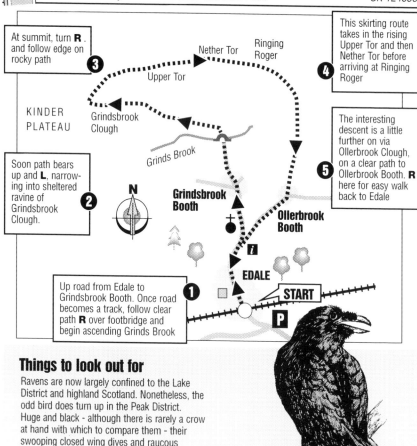

Stanage Edge 29

A linear walk, but none the worse for that. The famous climbing and beauty spot of Stanage Edge only comes into view after an interesting walk from Redmires Reservoir.

4 miles | 2 hours | None in area

Take a picnic | The Sportsman & Three Merry Lads | **P** Free public car park near Redmires Reservoir

MAP | Ordnance Survey Pathfinder number 743, Sheffield | *SK 256857*

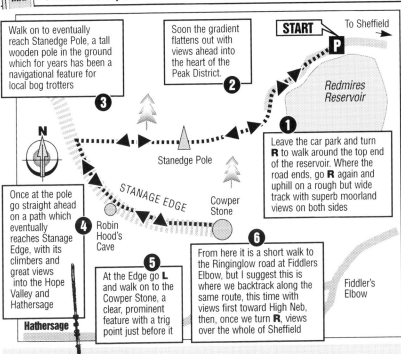

START To Sheffield

Redmires Reservoir

1 Leave the car park and turn **R** to walk around the top end of the reservoir. Where the road ends, go **R** again and uphill on a rough but wide track with superb moorland views on both sides

2 Soon the gradient flattens out with views ahead into the heart of the Peak District.

3 Walk on to eventually reach Stanedge Pole, a tall wooden pole in the ground which for years has been a navigational feature for local bog trotters

Stanedge Pole

STANAGE EDGE

Cowper Stone

Robin Hood's Cave

4 Once at the pole go straight ahead on a path which eventually reaches Stanage Edge, with its climbers and great views into the Hope Valley and Hathersage

5 At the Edge go **L** and walk on to the Cowper Stone, a clear, prominent feature with a trig point just before it

6 From here it is a short walk to the Ringinglow road at Fiddlers Elbow, but I suggest this is where we backtrack along the same route, this time with views first toward High Neb, then, once we turn **R**, views over the whole of Sheffield

Fiddler's Elbow

Hathersage

Stanedge Pole

Things to look out for

The Ordnance Survey map can't agree on spelling here, calling the Edge Stanage and the Pole Stanedge - what isn't in doubt is the grandeur of the view towards Hathersage. The area below the Edge is littered with grindstones awaiting removal to the "manufactories" of old Sheffield. And fly-tipping is a new phenomenon?

30 Carl Wark

A rocky trek over millstone grit, via grindstone quarries with spectacular views. Small children may find it too demanding - wear decent boots and avoid the walk in mist.

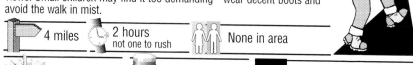

4 miles	2 hours *not one to rush*	None in area
Take a picnic	Fox House nearby	**P** At Surprise View, on A625

MAP | **Ordnance Survey Pathfinder 743: Sheffield** | *SK 252801*

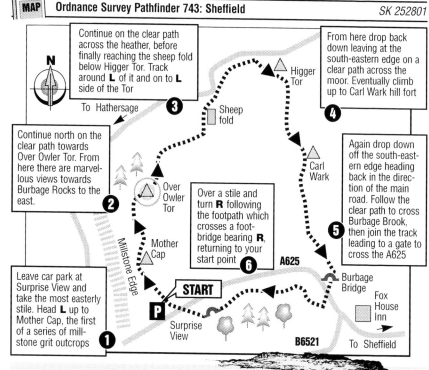

3 Continue on the clear path across the heather, before finally reaching the sheep fold below Higger Tor. Track around **L** of it and on to **L** side of the Tor

4 From here drop back down leaving at the south-eastern edge on a clear path across the moor. Eventually climb up to Carl Wark hill fort

2 Continue north on the clear path towards Over Owler Tor. From here there are marvellous views towards Burbage Rocks to the east.

5 Again drop down off the south-eastern edge heading back in the direction of the main road. Follow the clear path to cross Burbage Brook, then join the track leading to a gate to cross the A625

6 Over a stile and turn **R** following the footpath which crosses a footbridge bearing **R**, returning to your start point

1 Leave car park at Surprise View and take the most easterly stile. Head **L** up to Mother Cap, the first of a series of millstone grit outcrops

N · To Hathersage · Sheep fold · Higger Tor · Carl Wark · Over Owler Tor · Mother Cap · Millstone Edge · A625 · **START** · Surprise View · Burbage Bridge · Fox House Inn · B6521 · To Sheffield

Things to look out for

Star of this grand outing must the ancient hill "fort" of Carl Wark. Most experts reckon it dates back to pre-Roman times, probably the Iron Age - although it might well have been reinforced in the fifth century.
Sturdy walls are visible on three sides, and it is easy to see why in lawless times locals sought shelter there.

Burbage Rocks 31

This enjoyable walk offers tremendous views throughout and can be combined halfway with a visit to a famous local hostelry.

3 miles	2 hours	Fox House Inn
Fox House Inn	Fox House Inn	**P** Layby at Upper Burbage Bridge

MAP Ordnance Survey Pathfinder 743, Sheffield — *SK 262807*

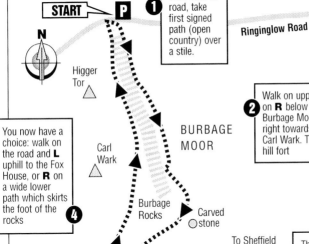

START **P** ❶ With back to road, take first signed path (open country) over a stile.

Ringinglow Road → To Sheffield

N

Higger Tor △

❷ Walk on upper path with the edge on **R** below the peaty plateau of Burbage Moor. Look constantly to right towards to Higger Tor and Carl Wark. The latter is an ancient hill fort

BURBAGE MOOR

Carl Wark △

❹ You now have a choice: walk on the road and **L** uphill to the Fox House, or **R** on a wide lower path which skirts the foot of the rocks

Burbage Rocks

Carved ◯ stone

To Sheffield
Fox House Inn **A625** →

To Hathersage

❸ This path finally descends when a large stone block, partially carved and then abandoned, comes into view. This marks a path dropping down **R**.

Things to look out for

While on this walk, and coincidentally enough considering the proximity of the pub, I saw a fox wandering along the lower path. From above its body seemed to run along the ground like water rather than a living creature and it seemed completely unconcerned by an angry crow which mobbed it on its way.

Fox House Inn and namesake

32 Mam Tor Circuit

This is a classic tour along one of the area's best ridges. Take care in frosty weather and avoid in mist. Views into the Edale Valley are superb.

5 miles	3 hours to enjoy views	In Castleton

Plenty in Castleton	Plenty in Castleton	**P** Large car park Castleton or Mam Nick picnic site

MAP Ordnance Survey Outdoor Leisure: The Dark Peak   *SK 151829*

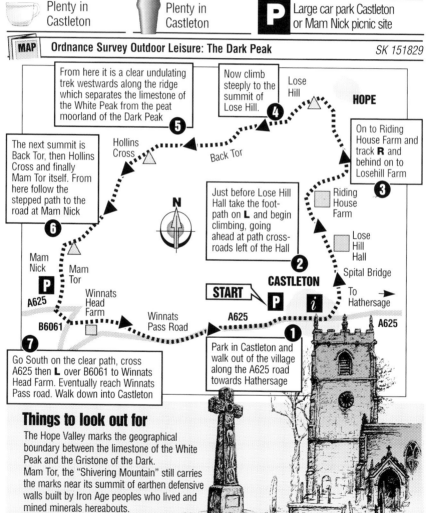

From here it is a clear undulating trek westwards along the ridge which separates the limestone of the White Peak from the peat moorland of the Dark Peak **5**

Now climb steeply to the summit of Lose Hill. **4**

Lose Hill

HOPE

On to Riding House Farm and track **R** and behind on to Losehill Farm **3**

The next summit is Back Tor, then Hollins Cross and finally Mam Tor itself. From here follow the stepped path to the road at Mam Nick **6**

Hollins Cross

Back Tor

Just before Lose Hill Hall take the foot-path on **L** and begin climbing, going ahead at path cross-roads left of the Hall **2**

Riding House Farm

Lose Hill Hall

N

Mam Nick **P**

A625

Mam Tor

Winnats Head Farm

B6061

7

Winnats Pass Road

A625

START **P** **i**

CASTLETON

Spital Bridge

To Hathersage

A625

Go South on the clear path, cross A625 then **L** over B6061 to Winnats Head Farm. Eventually reach Winnats Pass road. Walk down into Castleton

Park in Castleton and walk out of the village along the A625 road towards Hathersage **1**

Things to look out for

The Hope Valley marks the geographical boundary between the limestone of the White Peak and the Gristone of the Dark.
Mam Tor, the "Shivering Mountain" still carries the marks near its summit of earthen defensive walls built by Iron Age peoples who lived and mined minerals hereabouts.

Castleton

Rushup Edge 33

This is an exhilirating walk including a fine ridge, on good paths.
Avoid the Edge in mist, in high winds a parallel path beneath the Edge
might be favoured

5 miles	3 hours	Edale

Edale or take a picnic	Edale	**P** Car park in Edale

MAP Ordnance Survey Outdoor Leisure: The Dark Peak   *SK 124 853*

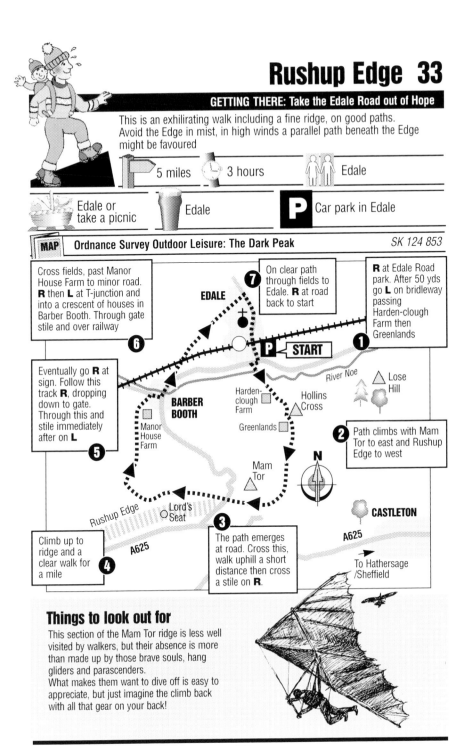

Cross fields, past Manor House Farm to minor road. **R** then **L** at T-junction and into a crescent of houses in Barber Booth. Through gate stile and over railway **6**

On clear path **7** through fields to Edale. **R** at road back to start

R at Edale Road **1** park. After 50 yds go **L** on bridleway passing Harden-clough Farm then Greenlands

Eventually go **R** at sign. Follow this track **R**, dropping down to gate. Through this and stile immediately after on **L** **5**

Path climbs with Mam **2** Tor to east and Rushup Edge to west

Climb up to ridge and a clear walk for a mile **4**

The path emerges **3** at road. Cross this, walk uphill a short distance then cross a stile on **R**.

EDALE

BARBER BOOTH

Manor House Farm

Harden-clough Farm

Greenlands

Mam Tor

Lord's Seat

Rushup Edge

A625

River Noe

Hollins Cross

Lose Hill

N

CASTLETON

A625

To Hathersage /Sheffield

Things to look out for

This section of the Mam Tor ridge is less well visited by walkers, but their absence is more than made up by those brave souls, hang gliders and parascenders.
What makes them want to dive off is easy to appreciate, but just imagine the climb back with all that gear on your back!

34 Hope Valley

GETTING THERE: On A625 between Hathersage and Castleton

This is a pleasant low-level wander along both sides of the Hope Valley, ideal even in December, when the tops can be shrouded in mist. Paths are clear, if sometimes muddy, throughout.

 3.5 miles 2 hours 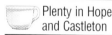 In Castleton

Plenty in Hope and Castleton

Plenty in Hope and Castleton

P Car park in village and spaces near front of church

MAP Ordnance Survey Outdoor Leisure: The Dark Peak *SK 173834*

Take a **R** turn at training centre and follow the lane (marked 'Rotary'). This track and later path leads to Losehill Hall **5**

Along the back of the hall and continue through fields. At a finger post for Mam Tor bear **R** slightly downhill and across a railway line via a bridge **6**

Continue straight ahead on path to finally reach the road at Killhill Bridge. **R** here and downhill back to start **7**

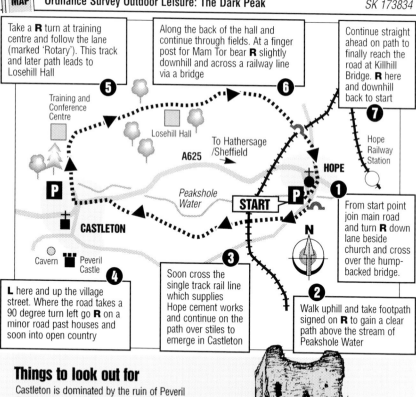

From start point join main road and turn **R** down lane beside church and cross over the hump-backed bridge. **1**

Walk uphill and take footpath signed on **R** to gain a clear path above the stream of Peakshole Water **2**

Soon cross the single track rail line which supplies Hope cement works and continue on the path over stiles to emerge in Castleton **3**

L here and up the village street. Where the road takes a 90 degree turn left go **R** on a minor road past houses and soon into open country **4**

Things to look out for

Castleton is dominated by the ruin of Peveril Castle built soon after the Conquest to keep the revolting Saxons in check.
The site is superb, controlling the valley linking Cheshire and Derbyshire, and well worth a walk up to the walls.
The property is owned by English Heritage who regularly host events in summer.

Roman Fort Walk 35

This is an interesting afternoon stroll along a quieter end of the Hope Valley, passing a fine pub and visiting an important historic site. Safe in all weathers.

 3 miles   2 hours   Hope

Hope, or take a picnic   Cheddar Cheese, Hope   Pay and display in village, or limited parking outside church

 MAP   Ordnance Survey Outdoor Leisure: The Dark Peak   *SK 193834*

2 At hamlet of Killhill Bridge bear **R** onto a lane (no through road sign). Ignore the first footpath and pass the house before going **R** on path to Aston

3 Under railway bridge to Fairfield Farm and road. **L** here and uphill. Follow road towards Aston

4 As road starts to drop, take path on **R** downhill, stream on **L**, to Hope Station via iron gate in the far left hand corner of field

5 Cross line via footbridge. At metalled track go **L** and soon after **R**, via another gate, on a path to A625

1 Take the minor road into the Edale Valley, passing the Cheddar Cheese Pub.

7 **R** on path through old Roman settlement of Navio. Straight on across several fields with boundary on **L**

6 **L** here for 100yds then cross road to stile and path close to river Noe, which leads to an ancient water mill at Brough. **R** over two footbridges beside road

8 Keep high, but follow path as it eventually wends downhill to road. **R** here, back into Hope

Things to look out for

Navio Roman site isn't the country's most revealing, an earthen bank and a description board is about all you get, but worth a visit nonetheless.

It is easy to see why the legions chose this point on the west-east salt route and for us to imagine how man has populated this valley for thousands of years.

Brough Water Mill

36 Beside the Derwent

GETTING THERE: Leave Hathersage on B6001 towards Grindleford

A delightful meander beside the infant River Derwent, on clear if somewhat muddy paths. Half way along, the river is crossed by stepping stones. These are easy, but take care in wet weather

 3 miles 2 hours None on route

Pub, Hathersage or take a picnic | Plough Inn

P Beside road or at pub (if you intend to patronise it)

MAP Ordnance Survey Pathfinder number 743: Sheffield

SK 234806

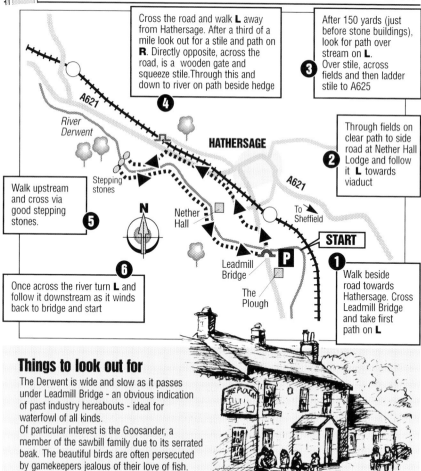

Cross the road and walk **L** away from Hathersage. After a third of a mile look out for a stile and path on **R**. Directly opposite, across the road, is a wooden gate and squeeze stile. Through this and down to river on path beside hedge **4**

After 150 yards (just before stone buildings), look for path over stream on **L**.
3 Over stile, across fields and then ladder stile to A625

River Derwent

HATHERSAGE

Through fields on clear path to side road at Nether Hall Lodge and follow it **L** towards **2** viaduct

A621

Stepping stones

Walk upstream and cross via good stepping stones. **5**

N

Nether Hall

To Sheffield

START

6 Once across the river turn **L** and follow it downstream as it winds back to bridge and start

Leadmill Bridge

The Plough

P

1 Walk beside road towards Hathersage. Cross Leadmill Bridge and take first path on **L**

Things to look out for

The Derwent is wide and slow as it passes under Leadmill Bridge - an obvious indication of past industry hereabouts - ideal for waterfowl of all kinds.

Of particular interest is the Goosander, a member of the sawbill family due to its serrated beak. The beautiful birds are often persecuted by gamekeepers jealous of their love of fish.

The Plough

Padley Gorge 37

This is a familiar area, but well worth a visit in the early summer thanks to the breeding birds which nest in the ancient woodland of the Gorge.

 4 miles 2 hours Grindleford Cafe (only if using cafe)

Longshaw Lodge, Grindleford Station Cafe, Fox House Inn

Fox House Inn, Grindleford Cafe

P Longshaw Lodge National Trust car park

MAP Ordnance Survey Outdoor Leisure: The Dark Peak   *SK 267801*

5 Follow riverside path up gorge, on **R** bank then over to **L** via footbridge and steps. **R** halfway up at path junction

6 Path crosses river and climbs uphill among trees to gate. Through gap beside it . **L** up road a few steps then cross it to Fox House Inn. Take path immediately across road from pub back towards Lodge and start

1 Walk downhill to Lodge and visitor centre, then **L** in front of Longshaw Lodge on a path beside ha-ha towards pond

Fox House

B6450

START

Longshaw Lodge **P**

Totley Tunnel

Padley Chapel

Pond

Grindleford Station Cafe

N

2 At pond turn **L** and walk straight ahead through grass dotted with pines to wide grass track. **L** here and over small stone bridge before **R** immediately after on narrow feint path

4 Path quickly descends to road. Cross this then **L** and **R** down to Grindleford Station and its famous cafe. Cross bridge over railway then **R** again through gap in wall

3 Through this to path along escarpment with wall on **L**

Things to look out for

This area is steeped in history, the latest addition being the Totley Tunnel - second longest in the country - which opens at Grindleford Station. Even more interesting is Padley Chapel, associated with the deaths of three Roman Catholics, the Padley Martyrs, who gave their lives for their faith at the end of the sixteenth century.

38 Froggatt Edge

GETTING THERE: A625 from Sheffield to Hathersage, then B6450 & B6054 to Froggatt

A classic edge walk with fine views across the valley. The second section is beside the River Derwent and then through ancient woodland.
Safe and full of interest for children.

 4 miles   2.5 hours   👥 None in area

☕ Grindleford   🍺 Several pubs on route   **P** At National Trust car park Haywood on B6054

MAP   Ordnance Survey Pathfinder Series: The White Peak   *SK 256778*

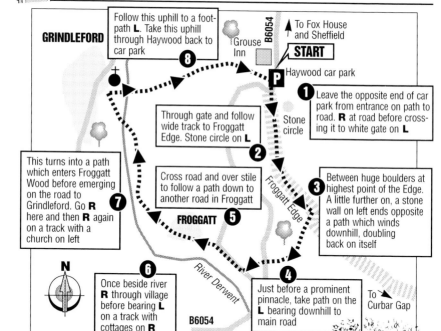

GRINDLEFORD

8 Follow this uphill to a footpath **L**. Take this uphill through Haywood back to car park

Grouse Inn

B6054

↑ To Fox House and Sheffield

START

Haywood car park

1 Leave the opposite end of car park from entrance on path to road. **R** at road before crossing it to white gate on **L**

2 Through gate and follow wide track to Froggatt Edge. Stone circle on **L**

Stone circle

3 Between huge boulders at highest point of the Edge. A little further on, a stone wall on left ends opposite a path which winds downhill, doubling back on itself

7 This turns into a path which enters Froggatt Wood before emerging on the road to Grindleford. Go **R** here and then **R** again on a track with a church on left

5 Cross road and over stile to follow a path down to another road in Froggatt

FROGGATT

N

6 Once beside river **R** through village before bearing **L** on a track with cottages on **R**

River Derwent

4 Just before a prominent pinnacle, take path on the **L** bearing downhill to main road

To Curbar Gap

B6054

Things to look out for

Froggatt Edge has many reminders of its ancient history, including the remains of a stone circle (right), but it is the climbing opportunities which make it popular these days.
Look out in spring for Cuckoos which perch on solitary trees, and for Dippers darting up and down the river - the latter identified by their white collars.

Historic Eyam 39

GETTING THERE: Leave Hathersage on B6001 and right past Grindleford

A relaxed ramble through rolling scenery on good paths, taking in the historic plague village. Avoid Eyam Moor in thick mist.

6 miles   3.5 hours   In car park

Plenty in village or take a picnic   Plenty in village   **P** Public car park in village

MAP   Ordnance Survey Outdoor Leisure: The White Peak   *SK 216767*

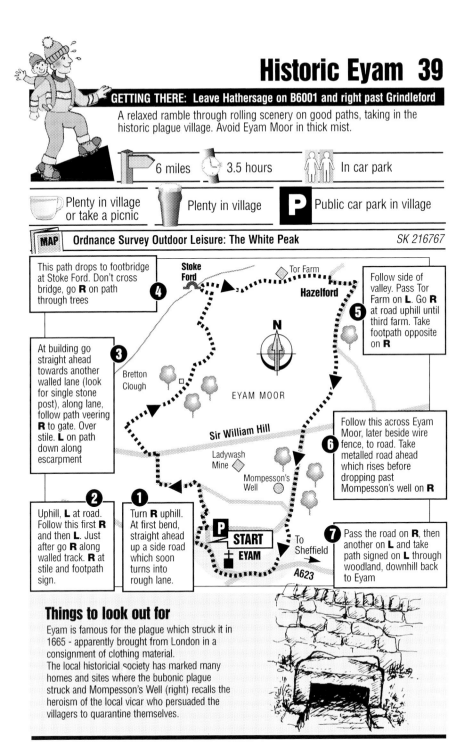

4 This path drops to footbridge at Stoke Ford. Don't cross bridge, go **R** on path through trees

Stoke Ford   Tor Farm   **Hazelford**

5 Follow side of valley. Pass Tor Farm on **L**. Go **R** at road uphill until third farm. Take footpath opposite on **R**

3 At building go straight ahead towards another walled lane (look for single stone post), along lane, follow path veering **R** to gate. Over stile. **L** on path down along escarpment

Bretton Clough

EYAM MOOR

Sir William Hill

Ladywash Mine

Mompesson's Well

6 Follow this across Eyam Moor, later beside wire fence, to road. Take metalled road ahead which rises before dropping past Mompesson's well on **R**

2 Uphill, **L** at road. Follow this first **R** and then **L**. Just after go **R** along walled track. **R** at stile and footpath sign.

1 Turn **R** uphill. At first bend, straight ahead up a side road which soon turns into rough lane.

P START † EYAM

To Sheffield

A623

7 Pass the road on **R**, then another on **L** and take path signed on **L** through woodland, downhill back to Eyam

Things to look out for

Eyam is famous for the plague which struck it in 1665 - apparently brought from London in a consignment of clothing material.
The local historical society has marked many homes and sites where the bubonic plague struck and Mompesson's Well (right) recalls the heroism of the local vicar who persuaded the villagers to quarantine themselves.

40 White Edge

GETTING THERE: B5064 from Sheffield towards Froggatt and Calver

This energetic tour takes in three of the Peak District's best known edges in a well trodden but enjoyable tour. Paths are good throughout, but avoid it in mist.

5 miles   3 hours   None on route

Grouse Inn or take a picnic   Grouse Inn   **P** Haywood car park on right just after Grouse Inn

MAP   Ordnance Survey Outdoor Leisure: The White Peak   *SK 256778*

① Head **R** on a path with wall on **R** then diagonally through fields to emerge at road near Grouse Inn

START   **P**

Grouse Inn   To Fox House

② Cross road and take signed path 50yds up the road. Cross a field to a gate in top left hand corner, then follow wall up to northern end of White Edge

⑥ This path emerges at road, which is crossed to a path opposite and back to start

B6054

Stone Circle

White Edge

③ **R** at finger post and walk for 1.5 miles along the edge. The path eventually goes **R** again at another finger post

Froggatt Edge

N

④ Downhill and over footbridge to car park at Curbar Gap. Through this and up steps on **R**, to join Curbar Edge path

Curbar Edge

⑤ This eventually becomes Froggatt Edge. Just before woodland look for ancient stone circle on **R**

P Curbar Gap

Things to look out for

This is lovely, wild moorland country, particularly the land north of White Edge. I once saw a female Hen Harrier in the area, although the much persecuted bird does not nest around here. The male is striking in its slate grey plumage, while the female is browner with distinct dark stripes across its long tail.

Three Edges Circuit 41

GETTING THERE: Head to Calver, between Grindleford & Baslow, then uphill to Curbar

This is a terrific walk along two fine edges and visiting two monuments to heroes from the Napoleonic Wars on the way. Do not attempt in mist.

5 miles	3 hours	At Robin Hood
Take a picnic	Robin Hood Inn	**P** Peak District car park at Curbar Gap

MAP Ordnance Survey Outdoor Leisure: The White Peak   *SK 262746*

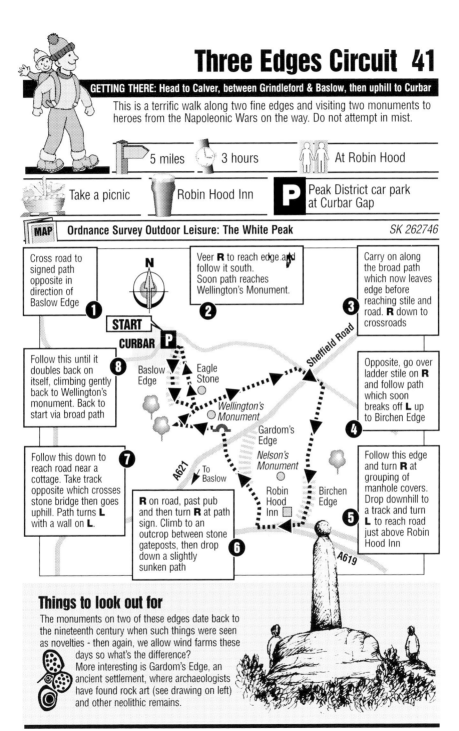

1 Cross road to signed path opposite in direction of Baslow Edge

START
CURBAR P

2 Veer **R** to reach edge and follow it south. Soon path reaches Wellington's Monument.

3 Carry on along the broad path which now leaves edge before reaching stile and road. **R** down to crossroads

8 Follow this until it doubles back on itself, climbing gently back to Wellington's monument. Back to start via broad path

Baslow Edge

Eagle Stone

Wellington's Monument

Gardom's Edge

Nelson's Monument

Sheffield Road

4 Opposite, go over ladder stile on **R** and follow path which soon breaks off **L** up to Birchen Edge

7 Follow this down to reach road near a cottage. Take track opposite which crosses stone bridge then goes uphill. Path turns **L** with a wall on **L**.

A621

To Baslow

Robin Hood Inn

Birchen Edge

6 **R** on road, past pub and then turn **R** at path sign. Climb to an outcrop between stone gateposts, then drop down a slightly sunken path

5 Follow this edge and turn **R** at grouping of manhole covers. Drop downhill to a track and turn **L** to reach road just above Robin Hood Inn

A619

Things to look out for

The monuments on two of these edges date back to the nineteenth century when such things were seen as novelties - then again, we allow wind farms these days so what's the difference? More interesting is Gardom's Edge, an ancient settlement, where archaeologists have found rock art (see drawing on left) and other neolithic remains.

42 North From Calver

This is a longer route than usual, making an ideal full day out. Half way is the village of Eyam with its hall, museum and welcoming pubs.

 6 miles   3 hours   Eyam, Stoney Middleton

Picnic, Calver, Eyam, or Stoney Middleton   Calver, Eyam, or Stoney Middleton   **P** Near church in Calver

MAP | Ordnance Survey Outdoor Leisure: The White Peak   *SK 247744*

5 Path reaches Eyam. Go towards centre. **L** up Lydgate and on towards buildings and path beside gate

4 Uphill again on clear path which soon enters woodland then veers **L** on a lane in direction of Eyam

Riley Graves

3 Up this field and next, to minor road. Through stile beside gate almost opposite

EYAM

Knouchley Farm

2 Follow to crossroad just after weir and on to Froggatt. At bridge go **L**. Up road to T junction. and across to stile opposite

Roman Baths

6 Over fields and then downhill towards track into Stoney Middleton. Follow this past church and the 'Roman Baths' spa house.

A623

STONEY MIDDLETON

Walk up Duke's Drive (opposite Bridge Inn). Pass Calver Mill before turning **L** on clear path beside the River Derwent

7 Soon after **R** at path sign over field. Halfway across, the path forks. Go **L** uphill to Knouchley Farm

N

8 **L** of buildings into lane down to road. Cross, down to river, turning **R**. At bridge take lane opposite, past bungalows, via fields back to Calver

Mill **1**

P Bridge Inn

CALVER   **START**

Things to look out for

The Riley Graves, a poignant reminder of the Eyam Plague are now in the care of the National Trust.

Holly abounds in the nearby woods. A closer look at trees growing above head height reveals leaves which are rounded rather than spiky - presumably if beyond the reach of grazing animals you don't need to protect yourself?

ALICE HANCOCK
BURAVG 9ᵗʰ1666

Foolow Round 43

This fine round walk reaches an escarpment where limestone meets gritstone and takes in grand views of those brave souls who glide from Great Hucklow.

4 miles   2 hours   None on route

Take a picnic   Pubs in Foolow & Great Longstone   **P** Park considerately in Foolow village

MAP   **Ordnance Survey Outdoor Leisure: The White Peak**   *SK 191768*

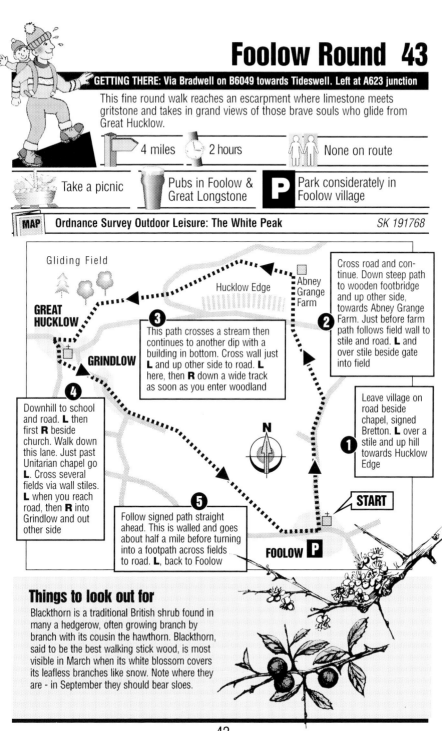

Gliding Field

Hucklow Edge

GREAT HUCKLOW

Abney Grange Farm

Cross road and continue. Down steep path to wooden footbridge and up other side, towards Abney Grange Farm. Just before farm path follows field wall to stile and road. **L** and over stile beside gate into field

3 This path crosses a stream then continues to another dip with a building in bottom. Cross wall just **L** and up other side to road. **L** here, then **R** down a wide track as soon as you enter woodland

GRINDLOW

4 Downhill to school and road. **L** then first **R** beside church. Walk down this lane. Just past Unitarian chapel go **L**. Cross several fields via wall stiles. **L** when you reach road, then **R** into Grindlow and out other side

Leave village on road beside chapel, signed Bretton. **L** over a stile and up hill towards Hucklow Edge **1**

N

5 Follow signed path straight ahead. This is walled and goes about half a mile before turning into a footpath across fields to road. **L**, back to Foolow

START

FOOLOW P

Things to look out for

Blackthorn is a traditional British shrub found in many a hedgerow, often growing branch by branch with its cousin the hawthorn. Blackthorn, said to be the best walking stick wood, is most visible in March when its white blossom covers its leafless branches like snow. Note where they are - in September they should bear sloes.

44 Miller's Dale

GETTING THERE: Monsal Head on B6465 from Wardlow

This is a popular circuit on good paths - an evening outing or one in winter might ensure a little more of the place to yourself.
Then again, it is easy to escape in the Peak Park.

 5 miles | 3 hours | Monsal Head

 Monsal Head, Litton Mill village | Monsal Head Hotel | **P** Behing Monsal Head Hotel (charge)

MAP | Ordnance Survey Outdoor Leisure: The White Peak | *SK 186714*

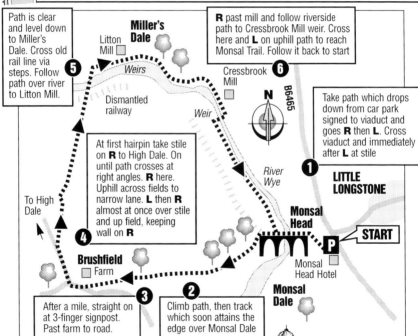

Path is clear and level down to Miller's Dale. Cross old rail line via steps. Follow path over river to Litton Mill. **5**

R past mill and follow riverside path to Cressbrook Mill weir. Cross here and **L** on uphill path to reach Monsal Trail. Follow it back to start **6**

Miller's Dale

Litton Mill

Weirs

Cressbrook Mill

Dismantled railway

Weir

Take path which drops down from car park signed to viaduct and goes **R** then **L**. Cross viaduct and immediately after **L** at stile

At first hairpin take stile on **R** to High Dale. On until path crosses at right angles. **R** here. Uphill across fields to narrow lane. **L** then **R** almost at once over stile and up field, keeping wall on **R** **4**

River Wye

LITTLE LONGSTONE

To High Dale

1

Monsal Head

START

Brushfield Farm

Monsal Head Hotel

After a mile, straight on at 3-finger signpost. Past farm to road. **3**

Climb path, then track which soon attains the edge over Monsal Dale **2**

Monsal Dale

Things to look out for

Miller's Dale, the beautiful gorge through which this walk travels, is filled by the waters of the River Wye which flows on through Ashford and then Bakewell. Look out for noisy Coot, with their white foreheads, and their smaller cousins, the Moorhens, with red bills.

Cressbrook Mill

Monsal Dale 45

A lengthy but undemanding walk down Monsal Dale. Return via rolling farmland. As well as a pleasant pub and superb view at Monsal Head, there is a craft centre and cafe in an old stable block.

 6 miles   3 hours   None on route

Monsal Head / Ashford   Monsal Head / Ashford   **P** Public Car Park behind Monsal Head pub

MAP   Ordnance Survey Outdoor Leisure: The White Peak   *SK 186714*

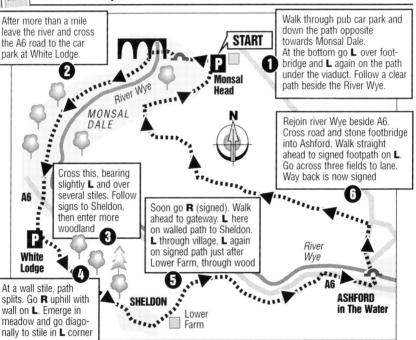

START

1 Walk through pub car park and down the path opposite towards Monsal Dale.
At the bottom go **L** over footbridge and **L** again on the path under the viaduct. Follow a clear path beside the River Wye.

2 After more than a mile leave the river and cross the A6 road to the car park at White Lodge.

River Wye

MONSAL DALE

N

6 Rejoin river Wye beside A6. Cross road and stone footbridge into Ashford. Walk straight ahead to signed footpath on **L**. Go across three fields to lane. Way back is now signed

A6

3 Cross this, bearing slightly **L** and over several stiles. Follow signs to Sheldon, then enter more woodland

P White Lodge

5 Soon go **R** (signed). Walk ahead to gateway. **L** here on walled path to Sheldon. **L** through village, **L** again on signed path just after Lower Farm, through wood

River Wye

4 At a wall stile, path splits. Go **R** uphill with wall on **L**. Emerge in meadow and go diagonally to stile in **L** corner

SHELDON

Lower Farm

A6

ASHFORD in The Water

Things to look out for

Monsal Head Viaduct once carried the railway between Manchester and the Peak.
These days it provides a welcome viewpoint for walkers who might be surprised to hear the abuse heaped upon such a stately structure by John Ruskin the Victorian aesthete and social campaigner. He has a museum dedicated to his work in Sheffield.

The Viaduct

46 Around Hassop

This walk takes in a fine pub with both excellent food and beer. The paths can be muddy in wet weather, so ideally opt for a cold, crisp winter's day.

 4 miles

2 hours

Only at pub

Eyre Arms

Eyre Arms

P Pilsley. Past pub and beyond the No Through Road sign

MAP Ordnance Survey Outdoor Leisure: The White Peak

SK 242711

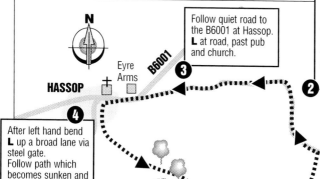

N

Eyre Arms

B6001

HASSOP

Follow quiet road to the B6001 at Hassop. **L** at road, past pub and church.

3

Cross road and over stile opposite. Up hill, tracking **R** and through a gate in corner. Stick to field boundary on **R** and straight ahead to reach minor road. **L** here

2

4

After left hand bend **L** up a broad lane via steel gate.
Follow path which becomes sunken and walled brefore crossing a stream and entering woodland

START

P Pub

Walk downhill, pass pub on **L** and over stile on **L** - barn opposite - and walk down field with wall on **R**. At wall end, over the two stiles on **R** . Diagonally down to cross small stream

1

5

PILSLEY

Through woodland and then pasture, reaching another road. Turn **R** Cross road when layby is reached and walk up hedge lined path to summit and then **L** back to start

Things to look out for

Hassop has a marvellous Roman Catholic Church, built by the family who owned the nearby hall.
Its Palladian entrance and grand honey coloured stone must have set the builder back a pretty penny but is well worth a look. Make sure you don't tramp mud inside!

Longstone Edge 47

GETTING THERE: B6001 from Calver crossroads, right to Gt Longstone at Hassop

This is as good walk for all the family with a bit of moderate climbing half way. The landscape hereabouts is interesting and typical of the limestone edges.

3 miles | 2 hours | None on route

Shops in village or take a picnic | Two pubs in Great Longstone | **P** Roadside in Great Longstone Please park considerately

MAP Ordnance Survey Outdoor Leisure: The White Peak | *SK 200708*

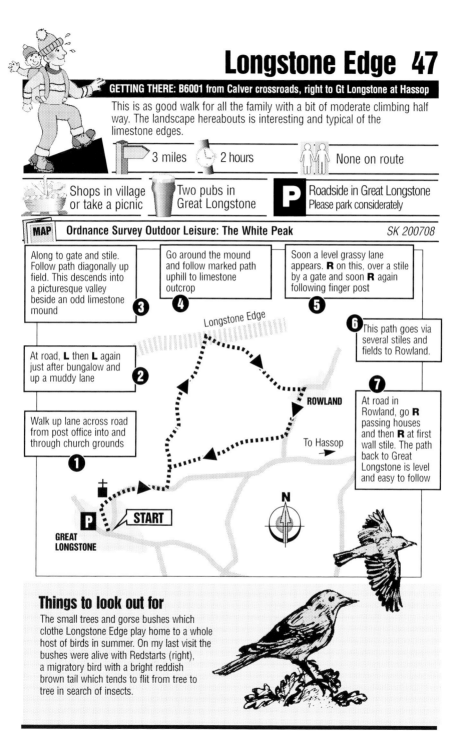

3 Along to gate and stile. Follow path diagonally up field. This descends into a picturesque valley beside an odd limestone mound

4 Go around the mound and follow marked path uphill to limestone outcrop

5 Soon a level grassy lane appears. **R** on this, over a stile by a gate and soon **R** again following finger post

Longstone Edge

6 This path goes via several stiles and fields to Rowland.

2 At road, **L** then **L** again just after bungalow and up a muddy lane

ROWLAND

7 At road in Rowland, go **R** passing houses and then **R** at first wall stile. The path back to Great Longstone is level and easy to follow

1 Walk up lane across road from post office into and through church grounds

To Hassop

P **START**

GREAT LONGSTONE

N

Things to look out for

The small trees and gorse bushes which clothe Longstone Edge play home to a whole host of birds in summer. On my last visit the bushes were alive with Redstarts (right), a migratory bird with a bright reddish brown tail which tends to flit from tree to tree in search of insects.

48 To Ashford

GETTING THERE: B6001 Calver to Bakewell Road

This is an easy ramble on good, albeit sometimes sticky, paths. Part of the route takes in the Monsal Trail which in Spring is filled with birdsong.

4 miles	2 hours	Bakewell, Ashford

Bakewell, Ashford or take a picnic	Plenty in Bakewell or Ashford	**P**	At former Hassop Station, next to Country Bookstore

MAP | Ordnance Survey Outdoor Leisure: The White Peak | *SK 218707*

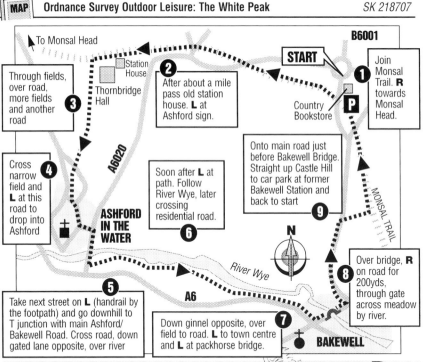

B6001

To Monsal Head

START

1 Join Monsal Trail. **R** towards Monsal Head.

Country Bookstore

Station House

2 After about a mile pass old station house. **L** at Ashford sign.

Thornbridge Hall

3 Through fields, over road, more fields and another road

A6020

4 Cross narrow field and **L** at this road to drop into Ashford

ASHFORD IN THE WATER

6 Soon after **L** at path. Follow River Wye, later crossing residential road.

Onto main road just before Bakewell Bridge. Straight up Castle Hill to car park at former Bakewell Station and back to start **9**

N

River Wye

5 Take next street on **L** (handrail by the footpath) and go downhill to T junction with main Ashford/Bakewell Road. Cross road, down gated lane opposite, over river

A6

7 Down ginnel opposite, over field to road. **L** to town centre and **L** at packhorse bridge.

MONSAL TRAIL

8 Over bridge, **R** on road for 200yds, through gate across meadow by river.

BAKEWELL

Things to look out for

Bakewell is perhaps well known enough to need little additional comment, but the complex of ancient structures near the A6 as we cross the Wye is remarkable. There is a narrow packhorse bridge (right) and close by a splendidly restored old sheep-dipping enclosure from the days when flocks were washed prior to market.

Wye Valley Round 49

An easy summer's day ramble with wonderful views in the first half. Ideal for families looking for exercise to go with the picnic. Why not take in Haddon Hall and make a day of it?

5 miles	3 hours	None on route

Bakewell, or take a pinic	Bakewell	**P** Public Car Parks in the centre of Bakewell

MAP Ordnance Survey Outdoor Leisure: number 24, The White Peak *SK 216685*

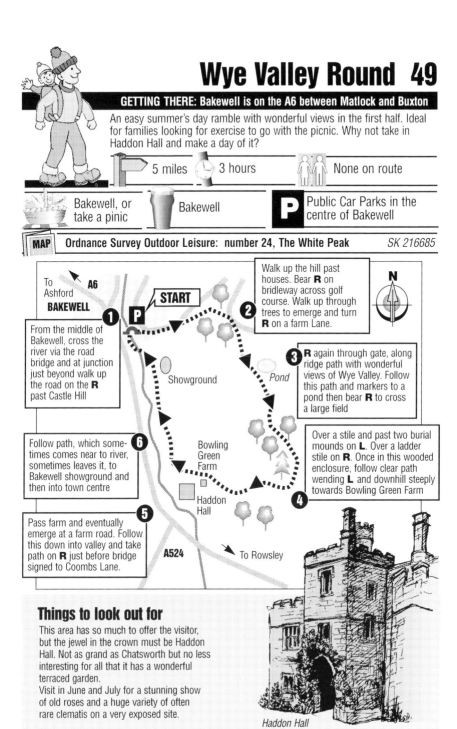

To Ashford **A6**

BAKEWELL

START

N

① From the middle of Bakewell, cross the river via the road bridge and at junction just beyond walk up the road on the **R** past Castle Hill

② Walk up the hill past houses. Bear **R** on bridleway across golf course. Walk up through trees to emerge and turn **R** on a farm Lane.

③ **R** again through gate, along ridge path with wonderful views of Wye Valley. Follow this path and markers to a pond then bear **R** to cross a large field

Showground

Pond

⑥ Follow path, which sometimes comes near to river, sometimes leaves it, to Bakewell showground and then into town centre

Bowling Green Farm

④ Over a stile and past two burial mounds on **L**. Over a ladder stile on **R**. Once in this wooded enclosure, follow clear path wending **L** and downhill steeply towards Bowling Green Farm

Haddon Hall

⑤ Pass farm and eventually emerge at a farm road. Follow this down into valley and take path on **R** just before bridge signed to Coombs Lane.

A524 To Rowsley

Things to look out for

This area has so much to offer the visitor, but the jewel in the crown must be Haddon Hall. Not as grand as Chatsworth but no less interesting for all that it has a wonderful terraced garden.
Visit in June and July for a stunning show of old roses and a huge variety of often rare clematis on a very exposed site.

Haddon Hall

50 Lower Lathkill Dale

GETTING THERE: A6 out of Bakewell and then B5056 to Alport

This popular circuit takes in a pub halfway and is quieter later in the year, away from summer crowds. Good paths in any weather

4 miles	3 hours	In Over Haddon
Take a picnic	Over Haddon	**P** In village on land near the bridge

MAP Ordnance Survey Outdoor Leisure: The White Peak   *SK 222646*

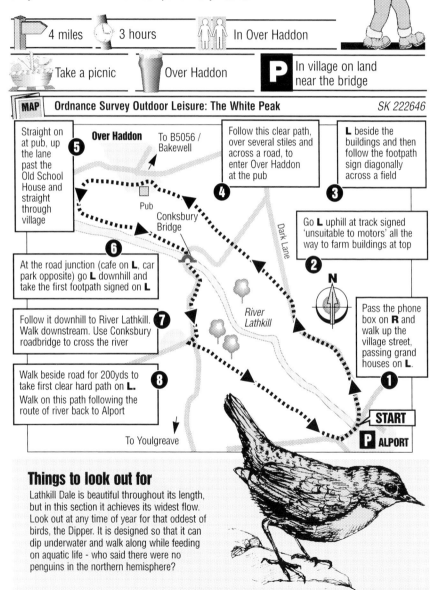

5 Straight on at pub, up the lane past the Old School House and straight through village

Over Haddon   To B5056 / Bakewell

Pub
Conksbury Bridge

4 Follow this clear path, over several stiles and across a road, to enter Over Haddon at the pub

3 **L** beside the buildings and then follow the footpath sign diagonally across a field

Dark Lane

2 Go **L** uphill at track signed 'unsuitable to motors' all the way to farm buildings at top

N

6 At the road junction (cafe on **L**, car park opposite) go **L** downhill and take the first footpath signed on **L**

River Lathkill

1 Pass the phone box on **R** and walk up the village street, passing grand houses on **L**.

7 Follow it downhill to River Lathkill. Walk downstream. Use Conksbury roadbridge to cross the river

8 Walk beside road for 200yds to take first clear hard path on **L**. Walk on this path following the route of river back to Alport

To Youlgreave

START

P ALPORT

Things to look out for

Lathkill Dale is beautiful throughout its length, but in this section it achieves its widest flow. Look out at any time of year for that oddest of birds, the Dipper. It is designed so that it can dip underwater and walk along while feeding on aquatic life - who said there were no penguins in the northern hemisphere?

White Peak Villages 51

GETTING THERE: A6 from Bakewell , then B5056 to Winster

A long but straightforward walk among the hills, dales and villages of the White Peak. Good, clear paths throughout, but children will find the distance too demanding.

9 miles	Allow all day	Youlgreave

Pubs/shops or take a picnic	Several on route	Birchover- near Druid Inn

MAP | Ordnance Survey Outdoor Leisure: The White Peak | *SK 238622*

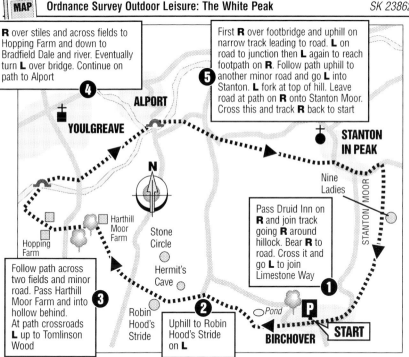

R over stiles and across fields to Hopping Farm and down to Bradfield Dale and river. Eventually turn **L** over bridge. Continue on path to Alport

❹

First **R** over footbridge and uphill on narrow track leading to road. **L** on road to junction then **L** again to reach footpath on **R**. Follow path uphill to another minor road and go **L** into Stanton. **L** fork at top of hill. Leave road at path on **R** onto Stanton Moor. Cross this and track **R** back to start

❺

ALPORT

YOULGREAVE

N

STANTON IN PEAK

Nine Ladies

Pass Druid Inn on **R** and join track going **R** around hillock. Bear **R** to road. Cross it and go **L** to join Limestone Way

❶

Harthill Moor Farm

Stone Circle

Hopping Farm

Follow path across two fields and minor road. Pass Harthill Moor Farm and into hollow behind. At path crossroads **L** up to Tomlinson Wood

❸

Hermit's Cave

Robin Hood's Stride

Uphill to Robin Hood's Stride on **L**

❷

Pond

STANTON MOOR

P

BIRCHOVER

START

Things to look out for

This area abounds in ancient history - and ancient myth. On this walk we pass the fabled Robin Hood's Stride, also known as Mock Beggar's Hall. Nearby is a stone circle complete with King Stone. Carved on the wall of once occupied Hermit's Cave is a crucifix. On our return we cross eerie Stanton Moor, complete with its own Nine Ladies Stone Circle and stunted oak and birch trees.

51

52 Around Hardwick Hall

GETTING THERE: Leave M1 South at Junct. 29 & follow signs for Hardwick Hall

This wander around the Hardwick Hall estate is a pleasant morning amble prior to visiting the property itself. The church at Ault Hucknall is a gem.

5 miles   2 hours   None on route

Hardwick Hall & Inn   Hardwick Hall Inn   **P** National Trust car park at Haddon Hall, next to Great Pond

MAP   **Ordnance Survey Pathfinder: Number 779, Mansfield (North)**   *SK 474636*

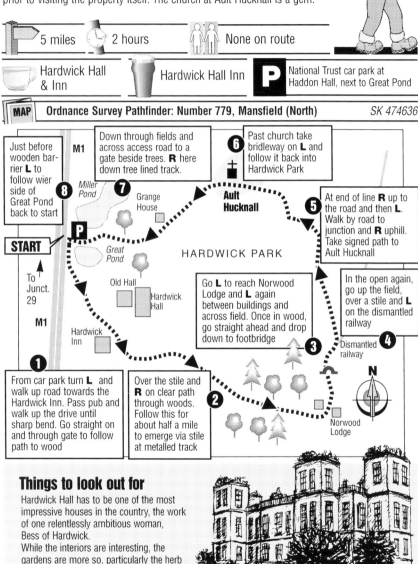

Just before wooden barrier **L** to follow wier side of Great Pond back to start

8 Miller Pond

M1

Down through fields and across access road to a gate beside trees. **R** here down tree lined track.

7 Grange House

Past church take bridleway on **L** and follow it back into Hardwick Park **6**

Ault Hucknall

At end of line **R** up to the road and then **L**. Walk by road to junction and **R** uphill. Take signed path to Ault Hucknall **5**

START

P

Great Pond

HARDWICK PARK

To Junct. 29

M1

Old Hall

Hardwick Hall

Go **L** to reach Norwood Lodge and **L** again between buildings and across field. Once in wood, go straight ahead and drop down to footbridge **3**

In the open again, go up the field, over a stile and **L** on the dismantled railway

Dismantled railway **4**

Hardwick Inn

N

1 From car park turn **L** and walk up road towards the Hardwick Inn. Pass pub and walk up the drive until sharp bend. Go straight on and through gate to follow path to wood

Over the stile and **R** on clear path through woods. Follow this for about half a mile to emerge via stile at metalled track **2**

Norwood Lodge

Things to look out for

Hardwick Hall has to be one of the most impressive houses in the country, the work of one relentlessly ambitious woman, Bess of Hardwick.

While the interiors are interesting, the gardens are more so, particularly the herb garden laid out as in Elizabethan times when it served as both supermarket and chemist shop.

Record sheet

Why not keep a note of which walks you do and when?

No.	WALK TITLE	Date	Who with	No.	WALK TITLE	Date	Who with
1	Ingbirchworth Reservoir			27	Kinder from the South		
2	Cannon Hall			28	Kinder Edge Walk		
3	Penistone Circuit			29	Stanage Edge		
4	Little Don			30	Carl Wark		
5	Langsett Moors			31	Burbage Rocks		
6	Wentworth Castle			32	Mam Tor Circuit		
7	Wentworth & Elsecar			33	Rushup Edge		
8	Scenic Bolsterstone			34	Hope Valley		
9	The Bradfields & Agden			35	Roman Fort Walk		
10	Grenoside Woods			36	Beside the Derwent		
11	Howden Edge			37	Padley Gorge		
12	Bradfield Moors			38	Froggatt Edge		
13	Dale Dike Circuit			39	Historic Eyam		
14	Sheffield & Tinsley Canal			40	White Edge		
15	Ulley Country Park			41	Three Edges Circuit		
16	Industrial Sheffield			42	North From Calver		
17	The Moss Valley			43	Foolow		
18	Redmires & Rivelin			44	Miller's Dale		
19	Redmires Circuit			45	Monsal Dale		
20	Mayfield Valley			46	Around Hassop		
21	Seal Stones			47	Longstone Edge		
22	Alport Castles			48	To Ashford		
23	Derwent Edge			49	Wye Valley Round		
24	Above Ladybower			50	Lower Lathkill Dale		
25	Ughill Moor & Strines			51	White Peak Villages		
26	Ladybower			52	Around Hardwick Hall		

Notes

Observations, comments, sketches, etc.